Dating For Women

Empowering Dating Advice For Women - Learn How To Easily Attract Men, Enjoy Better Relationships, Master Online Dating & Tinder, Find Love And Boost Your Confidence & Self Esteem

Kylie Bentley

© Copyright 2019 - All rights reserved.

It is not legal to reproduce, duplicate, or transmit any part of this document in either electronic means or in printed format. Recording of this publication is strictly prohibited and any storage of this document is not allowed unless with written permission from the publisher except for the use of brief quotations in a book review.

Table of Contents

Introduction 1

Chapter One: Why Modern Dating Is Challenging And How To Fix It 3

Chapter Two: Are You Dating Confident? 8

Chapter Three: How To Find The Perfect Partner 15

Chapter Four: The Art of Attraction 25

Chapter Five: Online Dating & Tinder: The Masterplan 34

Chapter Six: Dating Tips You Need To Know 44

Chapter Seven: Eight Easy Ways To Maintain And Improve Your Relationship 52

Chapter Eight: Seven Common Relationship Challenges (And How To Fix Them) 63

Chapter Nine: How To Date And Actually Enjoy It 75

Chapter Ten: How To Stay Safe Whilst Online Dating 84

Chapter Eleven: Does Mr. Right Really Exist? 92

Conclusion 100

Introduction

Finding that special somebody can be challenging, especially with the technological landscape changing the way we communicate with one another. Sometimes the relationship is reduced to brief stints of communication on a laptop or cellphone, making a real interaction less common but more valuable. However, relationships do not thrive without human interaction and connection. Clearly, relationships need a lot of work to survive and thrive. This book was created to help people with dating and relationships whilst staying relevant in today's Internet-savvy world.

Yet sometimes relationships deteriorate with the overuse of technology. For example, instead of having an animated conversation with an actual person, we substitute the cellphone for his or her words, reactions, and actions. However, technology like cellphones and laptops do not convey body language as innately as a human being. Yet one cannot blame technology as the sole source of dating and relationship difficulties either. In short, people can use technology to either enhance or undermine dating and relationships.

The main goal of this book is to help women use technology wisely to find a worthwhile relationship because let's face it, all the dating apps in today's world can be overwhelming and confusing. Yet they can also save you the hardship of expending the time, energy, and effort to meet and greet complete strangers. In other words, as numerous as dating apps are, they are also very specific in listing the characteristics and attributes of the soulmate you seek. Thankfully this allows you to get to know a person more than if you just met them on the street given characteristics listed in plain sight on the dating app.

This book offers some helpful tips and advice on how to negotiate the dating and relationship scene whilst boosting your confidence in doing so. For example, to be your best self one tip is to look within instead of looking to external sources for validation. Another tip is to be realistic in searching for a mate as compared to setting unrealistic expectations for yourself and your potential soulmate. You will find the best answers to all your questions about dating, the art of attraction, relationships, and how to boost your confidence in yourself amid all the dating apps today.

The benefits of this empowering book on all things concerning romance and love in a fast-paced technological world will make you feel secure and confident in your own skin as you apply the tips and advice abundantly within. For example, chapter one on modern dating suggests that trusting your instincts as compared to going with today's dating norms is overall a healthier choice. Chapter two on dating confidence gives you more actionable steps on how to feel good about who you are whilst seeking your soulmate. Every chapter of this book will not only open your eyes as to your dating and relationship quest, but it will also make you more aware of yourself.

It is not advisable to wait to read this empowering and knowledgeable book because your soulmate could pass you by if you do nothing. In addition, you will be missing out on how satisfying your life could be with a soulmate that truly understands, accepts, and loves you for who you are. You will not only find this book enriching your own life, but that of your potential soulmate as you apply the tips, advice, and steps towards a more fulfilling and romantic future for the both of you.

Chapter One: Why Modern Dating Is Challenging And How To Fix It

The pressure to be your best self and to find the perfect soulmate can be overwhelming. You have societal norms like dating apps which don't always make it easy. Societal norms like competition instead of cooperation can also make it challenging to make healthy choices when it comes to finding love. While some people prefer today's sketchy dating norms like benching, others prefer a more balanced approach to life and love. Even if you have to sift through many romantic profiles on Tinder, it is possible to find that special connection.

That special connection amid modern dating can be fraught with too much dependence on technology. Technology like the Internet making it possible to communicate without actually knowing the person in his or her real day-to-day life. In short, what you see on Match.com may not always be what you get because we often like to showcase our best self online which may not be representative of our true self. In the rare case of an online interest being representative of his or her true self, even then insecurities can arise. It seems more commonplace to the date below our standards because it is too intimidating to date an equal.

In short, double-standards can confuse things when it comes to modern dating. On the one hand, we want a successful partner who can hold his or her own. Yet we also want our significant other to be cooperative and reciprocal when it comes to the relationship. How can the modern woman have it all? She can start by being herself and not what society thinks she should be.

One part of being yourself is not feeling like you have to live up to some standard that isn't your own. For example, the dating standard/norm of having sex on the first date is not very wise nor realistic. Your potential soulmate might get the wrong impression, and you're left with the residual after-effects of a one-night stand, which can be even worse. Nobody wants to learn they are with a child a week later. Instead, why not take your time and get to know the person first?

Another modern dating norm I heard about at my previous job from a co-worker was about "catching feelings" about a man she was seeing casually. What is so wrong about having feelings for another person, anyway? Feelings aren't some type of disease you "catch," they simply are whether you want to acknowledge them on a first date or not. In fact, having feelings can help us build emotional connections that would not otherwise occur with cellphones and tablets. After all, cellphones and tablets and other technology are simply inanimate objects that can't love you back like a real person.

It just seems people don't follow traditional courting rituals anymore, given the Digital Age, and its counterparts like the Internet and dating apps more specifically. In short, knowing everything about a potential soulmate via his or her online profile on a dating app cannot take the place of organically meeting a person for the first time. One must consider words, reactions, and actions too. This body language is a better gauge of whether a potential soulmate more than likes you, in comparison to a smiley face on Facebook. Trust your gut instincts, they are usually right on.

Yet sometimes our natural intuition and innate instincts and feelings must be able to withstand a shot to the self-esteem amid the modern dating world because things can happen out of our control in the romantic sphere. For example, you get all ready to go out on your first date in months, only to get ghosted by a potential romantic interest. It can be challenging to realize it is nothing you did for this to happen. Just remember you are not responsible for somebody else's actions or inactions.

Actions sometimes do speak louder than words, especially when it comes to romantic intentions. More specifically, expecting a potential romantic interest to adhere to or follow modern dating norms is just unrealistic and unhealthy to some extent for both parties. For example, "friends with benefits" thing. Basically, it's like an understanding between two people to not become emotionally involved with each other but to still enjoy the sex. Yet that is just unsound and impractical because feelings will and do happen, eventually.

This is why we need to take care of ourselves amid the modern dating world. Things move and happen so fast in the Digital Age that it's hard not to get caught up in one of today's dating or relationship norms. That is when we step back and take a moment to assess the situation as objectively as we can. If the romantic situation does not seem healthy, safe, and sound, we must take actionable steps to either change the situation for the better or move on from the current situation.

The first step you can take is to take care of yourself, whatever that means for you. If it means taking a hot, relaxing bath or going out with your friends, do not hesitate. Sometimes a change of scenery or getting insight into the romantic situation from people who care about you can help. Taking care of yourself is utmost in priority.

The second step you can take is to be true to yourself, especially during a romantic date. During a romantic date, you don't want to let yourself be swayed or manipulated by something that doesn't feel or seem quite right. This is when listening to your instincts comes in handy to avoid being taken advantage of. Be genuine but not a victim. It would seem adhering to your own beliefs and values will help you succeed with your romantic date.

The third step you can take it to keep it real. What I mean is to not be something you are not. Don't be superficial in adhering to some romantic stereotype. In short, having the confidence to be yourself will also make you stand out and shine instead of being a wallflower. And let's face it, nobody wants to date a wallflower. It's okay to do you.

The fourth step you can take is to not get hung up on the small things. Instead of worrying what your friends and others may think of your newfound romantic interest and even yourself, just relax and let it flow. Don't worry if your hair and make-up are just right, because a genuine romantic interest will like you for you, and not what color your hair is or if you put foundation on today. Don't sweat the small stuff.

The fifth and most important step to take is to just relax and have fun! This is the most important step of all because what you don't want is to be so uptight and nervous that you don't give yourself any space to breathe and smile. You also don't want your romantic date to sense that you are unsure of yourself, because this will backfire possibly resulting in a less-than-positive outcome of the date and/or the potential future of the relationship. If you are certain of yourself, your romantic interest may sense your confidence, and that's just downright sexy!

Chapter Summary

In this chapter you have learned that even with all the current dating apps and resulting romantic trends, it is okay to take your time instead of feeling like you have to rush and make a choice already.

Taking your time is important because the romantic choices made in haste could affect the rest of your life, albeit positive or negative. When you take your time in dating and in choosing a significant other, you:

- Take care of yourself.
- Stay true to yourself.
- Keep it real.
- Don't sweat the small stuff.
- Relax and have fun!

There are also a few practical tasks you can take action on to make modern dating more applicable to your own life. These practical tasks will focus on what you can do right now to traverse the modern dating world. Since it would seem with modern dating that you have to be physically, emotionally, and mentally fit these days, you can exercise this trinity to improve your chance of surviving amidst modern virtual dating. For example, you can:

- Check out dating apps and websites..
- Research which dating app or website is best suited for you personally..
- Talk to others about their online dating stories and experiences.

In the next chapter, you will learn all about self-worth, self-esteem, and confidence when searching for potential romantic interest in today's Digital arena. You will learn things like the best advice and tips for having dating confidence. It is fairly hard to value your potential mate if you don't value yourself and know your own worth, to begin with. Putting stock in yourself will allow you to have the confidence to attract a potential mate. Then you can value both yourself and your significant other with love, care, and affection.

Chapter Two: Are You Dating Confident?

We all love to be confident in every aspect of our lives, whether that be work, friendships, or love. However, being a healthy person means sometimes being imperfect. That imperfection is what makes us human after all and is sometimes what even attracts a potential mate. Sometimes we fumble and that's okay. The important part is to pick yourself up and try again, especially in the romantic love sphere.

Being confident must start with you. Yet it can be challenging to have confidence when you have low self-esteem and self-worth. If you have been taught to value everything else like material things but not yourself, you wouldn't know much about valuing the beautiful person you already are, let alone valuing your potential romantic interest or significant other. This chapter will help you do just that by not only explaining why you should value yourself but also why it is a top priority in your life, especially your romantic life.

Sometimes we have to be our own date first and get to know ourselves even more before we even attempt to get to know somebody else. For example, take yourself out to somewhere you like or invest in a hobby you enjoy. Maybe step outside your comfort zone of who you believe yourself to be and explore new ways of being and thinking by getting to know people different from yourself. This can be helpful because when you gauge and understand your own reactions, feelings, and actions, you become more aware of yourself on a deeper level. Then you begin to trust yourself.

'Trusting' who you innately are means you slowly begin to develop self-worth and self-esteem over time in your abilities and capabilities, especially your capability to love yourself and even another. You begin to realize that you are enough, and anybody who

tries to imply otherwise is not worth your time, efforts, or energy. What is worth your energy, efforts, and time are investing in the beautiful person that is you. Once you invest in yourself on a continual basis, you can invest in and love somebody else in addition to yourself.

Self-love is vital.

Also, another vital aspect of today's fast-paced Digital World is maintaining 'self-respect'. Respecting yourself infers not letting people take advantage and walk all over you like a doormat, especially in a relationship. Self-respect also means you take care of yourself. If taking care of yourself means saying no or saying goodbye to a romantic love interest, then so be it. Sometimes it's better to be mindfully alone than to be with somebody who doesn't treat you with respect and consideration.

Sometimes the hardest thing to learn in any relationship is that how others treat and react to you may not be all about you. It is sometimes about them. For example, perhaps the potential romantic interest has emotional baggage from a previous relationship. This person may have a hard time differentiating between a past relationship and the present potential relationship. In this case, I would give the person space enough for him or her to get some closure first before even considering a romantic date or relationship.

However, sometimes it is about you. What I mean is you have to be realistic in your own expectations of yourself and of the potential love interest. If you are too busy with work, it would be hard to make room for an engaging relationship, anyway. If you are still dealing with past relationships and never got closure, it would be challenging to go into a new romantic relationship with an open mind as well. Being open to new experiences when meeting a potential love interest is also key.

Becoming dating material clearly takes a lot of commitment to yourself first. You must have the drive and the staying power to work on yourself continually and not just sporadically. With that being said, commitment could mean anything from going to the gym three times a week to pushing yourself to eat healthier to not spending money that could be put into savings. The point is you have to give a little to get a little.

However, it is important to not be too giving and revealing yourself on a first date. It is okay to talk about general interests, likes and dislikes that you and your potential love interest have in common. Yet I wouldn't reveal where I work right away nor where I hang out with my girls. Things could just get creepy if you do that because you may wind up with a stalker on your hands. Instead, why not keep things casual and meet at a public place you both agree on?

Another tip for going out on your first date is to just let it flow and happen naturally (within reason). Instead of trying to come at your potential love interest like the Spanish Inquisition in steering and controlling the conversation and situation, just listen and focus on what your date is saying and expressing. Don't listen to always have an answer, but mindfully pay attention to your date's words, reactions, and actions. The date will be more reciprocal between you both than one person doing all the heavy-lifting. In short, relationships are about mutual give-and-take.

A special shared relationship will also happen more naturally if you steer clear of engaging in head games. Both of the sexes can be guilty of this, especially when we think only of ourselves. Yet manipulation is bad for any relationship, especially romantic. If you are searching for a life partner, it is not advisable to engage in romantic affairs like a competition to win, because you will ultimately lose a lot more than you realize after the fact. In other words, romantic relationships are not some sport in which you go all in it to win it.

The only thing competition should be good for is sports, not love. You should never compare yourself to other women or men period, let alone on a date. Especially past dates and relationships because you will only end up letting yourself, and your potential romantic love interest, down. If you don't feel good enough to be there, to begin with, how can you feel you deserve the other party's time and affections? You'll be too focused on your own shortcomings to even notice.

What you should notice is how you respond on a date. If you're burnt out on the whole dating scene, especially with all the matchmaking websites and services out there, you won't give your potential love interest your full attention. Then he or she might think you are not interested when you really are. This could potentially push the person away. In short, the most important action you can take when dating is to give your potential love interest your valuable time and attention. This is priceless.

The worst thing you can do on a date is to pay more attention to your cell phone or another electronic device. This infers to your date that you are not as interested as he or she thought when you swiped left on that popular dating app a week ago. It is insensitive, indifferent, and just plain rude. Don't text and chat with your friends when you have a new date sitting right in front of you. Instead, why not put the cell phone away, make eye contact, and smile?

Communication is vital on a first date and in a romantic relationship. One form of communication that can say more than your words is body language. If your eyes are darting elsewhere, that tells your date you are either bored or not interested. However, if you are leaning into the conversation, making eye contact, and listening intently to every word your date utters, this says I'm into you. It is ok to flirt as well.

Moves, like brushing your hand against his and smiling with your entire demeanor, sends the signal that you are clearly attentive, engrossed, and intrigued. Another move you could do is to coyly or playfully bat your eyes and quickly look down. Most guys find this attractive and might also make a move in response like smiling at you directly. You want positive and possibly flirty actions and reactions on a date because this kind of information will tell you if you're moving in the right direction or not.

What may work for you on a first date may not work for everybody though, especially if you are trying to get to know somebody for the first time. We are all individuals with different needs and wants. Even so, there is no denying the universal need for a close emotional connection. We are all social creatures wanting and deserving of affection and attention. As a result, we must pay attention to today's dating norms although I argue the tried-and-true courting practices of the past are even more relevant as a result of them.

Chapter Summary

In this chapter, you have learned how important it is to be dating confident as compared to the opposite. Dating confident means you trust in yourself and have faith in the process whilst giving yourself room and space enough to make mistakes and breath. We all learn how to be dating confident through examples and sometimes even past failed dates and relationships. It is important to learn what to do as it is to learn what not to do. In any case, here are the main points from this chapter to consider:

- Being confident starts with you.
- Be your own first date!
- Trust yourself.
- Self-love and self-respect are vital.
- Be realistic.

- Be open to new experiences.
- Take care of yourself.
- Don't reveal too much, leave a little to the imagination.
- Let it happen naturally.
- Don't compare yourself to others.
- Give your date your full attention.
- Communicate!

There are also a few practical tasks you can take action on to ensure you are dating confident. These practical tasks will focus on what you can do right now to make dating confidence more a reality. For example, you could engage in a sport you enjoy like basketball or swimming to feel physically fit and more confident in your abilities and body image. You could also socialize with people to gain confidence in your social skills. You could even read up on current dating trends. In short, you can:

- Work on body image and confidence by joining a gym or team sport.
- Work on social skills by getting out and socializing more..
- Read up on current dating trends.

In the next chapter, you will learn how to find the perfect partner with sound suggestions from real-life experiences. You will also learn that while the perfect partner is out there, you also have to put in a little effort to be Ms. Right as well, for the door swings both ways. Mr. Right just won't come to you, you also have to put yourself out there as well. In short, meet him or her halfway. Do the work to get from point A to point B and have fun!

Chapter Three: How To Find The Perfect Partner

When it comes to searching out your potential romantic interest and possible lifelong partner, sometimes current social trends like matchmaking websites and dating apps don't always appeal to everybody. This is when you try to return to the fundamentals of dating in actual life, as compared to dating online. In real life, you wouldn't expend your energy hopping from one fling to the other simply because you thought he or she was attractive from his or her online profile. Instead, you would take the time to find out more about the person by organically asking them questions offline, compared to already knowing the answers ahead of time. This way you avoid sizing the person up before you actually get the chance to know him or her.

Instead of using a dating app to send a stereotypical text in an attempt to ask somebody out, I think it takes more courage to approach a potential love interest and ask him or her out in real life. In short, hiding behind our electronics do not work when we want to show and convey a genuine interest in somebody. Case in point electronics is not an extension of our person, and should not be treated as such when trying to approach somebody in an authentic and genuine way.

My husband with whom I have been together with for seven years took his time approaching me and did not use a dating app in the attempt to find out more about me. He took me out for coffee and we experienced real conversations about life and what not, as opposed to sending choppy text messages back and forth in broken English with a cute emoji. We went out on dates like real people to learn more about one another, not to gauge whether the other was a potential life partner from the get-go. It would appear that when dating in real life, it is important to take your time and don't go into it with preconceived notions and assumptions.

People still go out to meet people in the real world too, as compared to staying home on a Friday night in your comfy pants. The trick is to go places where you think your potential romantic interest could already be as a result of your own interests and hobbies, and I don't mean the typical dance clubs. Try someplace less expected, like an art exhibit or even the grocery store. If you know what you are looking for in a potential mate, you will also know where to go to fulfill the quest for love. This will be easier than if you went into it blindly.

With that being said, it is also important to be aware of your actions and inactions. If you are too busy texting a friend, you might not notice that attractive man reading a book at the table next to yours in the cafe. You might also be impervious to your surroundings, so take care to be aware. On that note, it is alarming to see people walking around with their cellphones in tow and staring at the device in their hands instead of interacting with the organic environment. Put the cell phone away and look around every once in a while.

There is clearly more to life than that popular dating app you are staring at on your cell phone. All you need to do is be alert with an open mind to really see it. In short, sometimes it is important to think outside the box when it comes to dating and meeting people because not everyone is impressed with the same stereotypical rituals and norms. While some potential love interests might prefer the typical dinner and a movie, others like to go to a bonfire and hang out with friends in common. And that's okay.

Having the courage to be yourself in a world of ever-changing dating norms is invaluable. Even if the potential love interest does not work out, you still have you at the end of the day to deal with, so don't fall victim to some dating fad when it really isn't you, to begin with. In other words, don't compromise who you really are for love. Stay true to yourself and others will notice your confidence to do you.

Yet finding the perfect partner also means you have to compromise sometimes to make it work. Everything is not going to go your way all the time. In addition, every once in a while you have to bend or sway to the other person's needs and wants before your own and vice versa. It's all about balance, reciprocity, and a mutual interdependence which is healthy.

Also healthy in finding the perfect partner for you is to not expend so much energy looking and searching for him or her. It will happen naturally when you least expect it, and you might just be surprised as a result. Instead, focus some of that boundless energy on yourself meanwhile because you should be settled or grounded in yourself and with your life goals before your potential love interest comes along and sweeps you off your feet.

Finding Mr. or Ms. Right and then falling in love shouldn't be such a task that you hardly have the time or energy left to enjoy the experience. The experience of finding the perfect partner should be fun and not a chore on a to-do list like grocery shopping. Nobody wants to feel like a chore or nuisance by asking of your time and energy. Yet Mr. Right might just slip away if you can't give him what he or she deserves to begin with. Your time and energy are more priceless than any material thing.

If your potential love interest tries to overcompensate with material gifts, it might incline you to think that the person doesn't feel adequate enough of their own merit, to begin with. Mr. or Ms. Right will innately know when you are trying to substitute material possessions for love, which never works in the long run. Such gifts might impress at first, but the newness of receiving a material gift eventually dissipates, and what happens if your suitor's feelings for you also dissipate after the newness wears off? Steer clear of confusing gifts for love.

Finding Mr. or Ms. Right is the gift in itself, and nothing else is needed. Gifts are nice, but they cannot respond to you the way your potential love interest or significant other can. The best gift of all is freely receiving your perfect partner's affections and love without conditions, and no gift can compete with that. Period.

It seems the only person you can compete with when trying to find the perfect partner is yourself because we are always trying to improve to become a better version of ourselves than we were yesterday. If not for ourselves, then for others we love and care about. Yet what if Mr. or Ms. Right thinks we are perfect just the way we are? Do not doubt yourself in trying to live up to your standards and goals because your perfect partner may sense your wavering and look for another naturally perfect mate. Be that as it may, sometimes perfection is overrated, especially when you are trying your best to be yourself, perfectly imperfect as you are.

The perfect partner will not care if you are fifteen pounds overweight or if you drink too much coffee. What he or she will care about and notice is if you are comfortable in your own skin. Comfortable enough to be yourself. When you are accepting of yourself, you are also more accepting of your perfect romantic partner. This includes acceptance of each other's strengths and weaknesses too.

Acceptance will help you in your quest for the perfect partner which will hopefully result in success, especially if you can find somebody with similar tastes, likes, and beliefs. It will then be easier to relate to your perfect partner as you will have things in common.

Yet sometimes opposites do attract as well, especially if there is a strong connection between you two love birds. And instead of finding differences intimidating, your perfect partner will find them enchanting and unique as he or she accepts you for who you are. This includes the entire package that is you, flaws and everything.

Yet sometimes in order to attract the perfect partner, we need to work on our flaws and issues first. If you are already needy and clingy, finding the perfect partner will not change that. That is when we need to get outside help like a friend or counselor to help us understand, modify, and improve our behavior, attitudes, and life outlook. For example, if you have issues letting go of a past romantic relationship, talking to a professional may not be such a bad idea. After all, that's what they are for.

Also there for you in your quest for finding Mr. Right are your friends and family. Talk to them to learn what their experiences are with finding the perfect partner. You may be surprised at what you may learn, and maybe some of that advice will also apply to your quest in finding Mr. or Ms. Right. For example, my uncle says to throw dating conventions out of the door because the time you used to court him you could have been used it to have fun without the pressure of impending romantic promises on the table. Sometimes we have to toss dating conventions by the wayside.

If you go into your quest for the perfect partner in thinking you may get something out of it, then you may be let down. Any self-fulfilling prophecies or motivation you have should be left at the door, in part because people will sense and pick up on your motivations and intentions eventually, anyway. Don't be a gold-digger always looking for the bigger, better deal. That will turn your potential perfect partner off and have lasting consequences.

What you do want to last is your perfect partner's feelings about and towards you, so don't do anything to put that in jeopardy. If it's meant to be, it's meant to be, so don't manipulate his or her feelings. Instead, try to nurture and cultivate your potential perfect partner's feelings about something he or she cares about into something healthy. This shows your potential perfect partner that you care for more than yourself in taking the time to foster emotional growth thereby empowering that emotional connection to come to fruition.

Such qualities and attributes are priceless in a world of individuality and competition to find the perfect partner whether online or offline. In a world of me, me, me, finding the perfect partner or love can sometimes seem a paradox. This is mainly because although it takes two to have a healthy relationship, a relationship with the perfect partner isn't all about one partner or the other. It is about both working together as two grown consenting adults.

If the perfect partner you seek is mature, he or she will be upfront and direct with you and not engage in immature games of the heart. The perfect partner will not lead you on and instead tell you how he or she really feels. The perfect partner will not only be honest with you from the get-go but also sincere in his or her intentions towards you. Likewise, you should be the perfect partner and reciprocate. It shows you are observing and listening intently to everything your potential perfect partner expresses and believes from the heart, and that is a turn-on.

In addition, another turn-on to your perfect partner is your thoughts on things that really matter to you. Don't be afraid to express your beliefs and opinions, because there is more to a relationship than physical assets. There is also intelligence and one's wit. These attributes are downright sexy in an age of monkey see monkey do. It is refreshing to witness one thinking for him or herself, and wit is incredibly stimulating and attractive.

Also attractive to your perfect partner is your ability to let him see that you are fallible and human after all. It is okay to make a mistake. We all do every once in a while. Just don't make the same ones repeatedly. Instead, learn from them, and your perfect partner will see that you can indeed grow as a person instead of staying dull and stagnant.

As long as your perfect partner sees you are trying, he or she will be proud of and possibly even more attracted to you regardless of the outcome. Your potential perfect partner will see you are indeed making an effort, and that will have a positive effect on the budding relationship, whether during a date or otherwise. Making the effort suggests to your potential perfect partner that you do not take things for granted and are willing to make improvements. It also infers you are flexible and open to suggestions.

One final suggestion to finding the perfect partner is to not sit and wait around for him or her to come to you. You have to put yourself out there as well. Meet your potential perfect partner halfway, as compared to sitting around and doing nothing. This will not only impress him or her, but it will also suggest you are ready for a possible relationship.

Chapter Summary

In this chapter, you have learned how to search out, find, and attract the perfect partner through specific actions in contrast to inaction. You have learned that while it is important to be yourself, you also have to put in a little effort to be your best self and improve daily. You have also been well-informed that dating offline organically is quite different from dating online. To each his or her own, but it seems some things remain consistent like your perfect partner's inclination to love you for who you are. In short, you won't have to second-guess if your perfect partner is really into you with all the tips and advice in this chapter.

Some key points to revisit about finding the perfect partner are:

- Offline dating and courting are more authentic and genuine.
- Leave your preconceived notions and dating conventions at the door.

- Go socialize and hang out someplace less expected to meet Mr. Right.
- Give Mr. Right your time and energy.
- Stay true to yourself but work on your flaws and interests.
- Be happy and satisfied with what you already have.
- Just let it be; if it's meant to be, it's meant to be.
- Be honest, upfront, and straightforward.
- Avoid playing games.
- Apply your intelligence and wit and think for yourself.
- Be willing to learn from your mistakes.
- And just try your best!

There are also a few practical tasks that you can take action on to find the perfect partner on your own life. These practical tasks will focus on what you can do right now to make finding the perfect partner more a reality. For example, you can join an offline group in something you are interested in like a hobby, craft, or organization. In short, this makes it more possible to find your perfect partner because he or she might have similar interests in the same thing. Some more practical tasks you can undertake to finding the perfect partner are:

- Ask friends and family to help you in your mission of finding the perfect partner.
- Invite people over for informal get-togethers like a bonfire with friends of friends.
- Join a bigger community to meet new people like the Red Cross.

In the next chapter, you will learn the art of attraction. More specifically, you will learn what moves to make to incline your perfect partner to seek a second date and to be more interested in you. You will also be well-informed as to what is sexy and what is not according to both sexes. So ladies and gents, get ready to flaunt it!

Chapter Four: The Art of Attraction

The art of attraction evokes interest in the other party through actions, words, and reactions. Although the art of attraction does happen naturally and instinctively, sometimes it also takes a little effort to woo your potential love interest. The results of putting in a little effort to attract your potential love interest will go a long way as he or she reciprocates your interest through his or her own actions, words, and reactions to you and your efforts. And nothing can compare to a mutual attraction between two love birds.

The attraction is like a pull or force of two magnets being drawn to one another as they move closer together. They are innately drawn to each other as they each move towards the other. No matter what you are initially attracted to in your potential love interest, you will find that this force of nature inclines you to want to be closer to him or her. You will find your desire for your potential love interest increasing as he or she pulls you in with his or her appealing nature.

You will also find that what appeals to one person may not appeal to the next. One person may like physical attributes more like pouty lips while the other may go more for intelligence and wit. Still, others may go for personality. Be that as it may, the attraction itself does not change despite what initially pulls you in. It is the entire package of physical, emotional, and intellectual attributes, not just one characteristic of the potential love interest.

However, sometimes one display of a singular sexy characteristic is all it takes to attract a potential love interest. He or she may like the way you smile or the way you look in a pair of jeans. Your potential love interest may even like your tastes in music, food, or even recreational activities and hobbies. Whatever attracts you two love birds initially is only the beginning of the connection. In addition, your potential love interest will find the confidence you display to be yourself more than appealing.

Also appealing is your beauty, and not just external beauty either. I'm talking internal beauty that only you possess just by being you. From the way you move to the way you pour your heart into something. That is beauty in of itself. However, sometimes we could all use a little help to attract a potential love interest.

The makeup you wear both for yourself and your potential love interest should only enhance your features and not blow them out of proportion to the rest of your face. Don't pile on the foundation or blush or eyeshadow, you will look too made up and potentially turn off your potential love interest. If you need a chisel to take off your makeup, you are putting one way too much of it. Instead, try to accentuate your features with more natural-looking makeup.

The clothes you wear should also enhance your natural figure within reason. Don't adorn clothes that make you look cheap and sketchy. Instead, wear clothes that leave a little something to the imagination. Also, adorn clothes that emphasize your best features. If you are all legs, wear jeans for instance

A sense of smell is also important when it comes to attracting a potential love interest. Whether you choose to wear cologne or perfume, is up to you. However, because some love interests already like your natural scent, you might not need a lot of fragrance or any fragrance at all. Don't over-power your potential love interest with too much fragrance that he or she chokes on it. Sometimes a good bar of soap is all you really need.

Good self-grooming clearly attracts a potential mate. In short, people like people that take care of themselves. So be sure to shower and get a haircut. For ladies, please shave your legs. Nobody wants to date Magilla Gorilla.

The art of attraction is more than external appearances and scent. It is also about inherent beauty that each one of us possesses and displays just by being ourselves. Yet in addition to being yourself to attract a potential love interest, you have to be your best self. Being your best self could mean a number of things.

To be your best self means sometimes you have to invest in yourself. Investing in yourself could mean you eat a healthier diet or it could mean you take a fun class to learn a new hobby that you and your potential love interest might enjoy and benefit from. Benefitting both love birds is also investing in exercise because when you are in better physical condition, you are able to do more activities with your potential love interest. However, investing in yourself could also mean you work on your shortcomings so that when you are ready to meet a potential love interest, you can focus more on your date and not your hang-ups.

Investing in and working on yourself also suggests you don't already think you are perfect, and your potential love interest will like that you see there is always room for improvement. It will suggest you are humble, modest, and hard-working as well. It also suggests you have something more to offer your potential love interest, because if you are already perfect, what could you potentially have to offer that hasn't already been perfected and consequently finished? It suggests you are not lifeless and stagnant and that you are willing to try. In short, you got flow and game, and that my friend is attractive.

The attraction is like an art form that requires a patient artist to create the masterpiece with careful attention to detail. In short, you must sometimes paint a picture for the other party to take a hint (as opposed to chucking a brick at them). Sometimes that requires the artful finagling of details like the setting for sparks to occur. Other times, the art of attraction requires only one detail to change the entire picture like the color of your hair or a certain look in your eyes. The art of attraction could potentially create a masterpiece in you.

Clearly, the art of attraction takes time and patience. Similarly, the art of attraction can also be like the creation of fine wine. Sometimes the wine aficionado has to allow the carefully selected ingredients to meld before the final product is ready. Likewise, your potential love interest may need time to blend and combine your fruitful attempts to attract his or her attention. Don't give up and keep trying to win your potential love interest over.

It goes without saying that being positive about the whole experience can also attract a potential love interest. If your mood or state of mind is negative, it will be fairly challenging to attract your potential love interest. You attract what you give out. So do the things that make you happy. As a result, you will be more attractive, not only to yourself but to your potential love interest.

The art of attraction is clearly a two-way street because while one party is making the moves, the other is the recipient of those sexy moves. It is a give and takes in which the art of attraction is interactive and ongoing. It is never dull and lifeless. Instead, the art of attraction is full of energy, vitality, and dynamic. It is life itself because everything is attracted to something. Why else would there even be a so-called "Law of Attraction" if this weren't the case?

The Law of Attraction basically states that whatever the mind can conceive and believe, it shall achieve. So if you have thoughts about attracting your potential love interest, it will happen. If you believe you can apply your powers of attraction to pull in closer your potential love interest, you will have a better chance at succeeding than if you don't believe it. In short, if you have trust and confidence in yourself, it will happen.

What might also happen when you apply and use the art of attraction is you might attract a few frogs before finally finding your prince charming. And that's okay. At least this way you get some experience and learn what you find attractive and not attractive as well. In addition, you learn what works and doesn't work when it comes to attracting your potential love interest.

Yet with the art of attraction, there is a fine line between wooing your potential love interest and playing games. In short, while it is okay to use the art of attraction, it is not okay to abuse the art of attraction. The difference is when you manipulate your potential love interest by overdoing specific aspects of the art of attraction like using your "assets" to get what you want without considering the other party. Don't do that. Guys see through that anyway.

What you can do in lieu of the art of attraction is to use it wisely. Don't try to control the outcome of your first date with your potential love interest. In other words, go with the flow. If your potential love interest senses your attempts are somewhat forced, he or she might pull away. And that is what you don't want. Let things develop naturally.

Naturally, the art of attraction is easier for some women than it is for others. If that is the case, take the time to observe the women whom you aspire to be like and perhaps learn from them. Maybe even embrace or espouse what works for them and try it yourself. You may be pleasantly surprised at the outcome.

Yet the point of attraction and a first date is to not focus on the outcome, and instead mindfully be in the moment. Take notice of your potential love interest's reactions and actions in response to your attempts to flirt and attract him or her. Also, take note of your own reactions and actions in response to your potential love interest's attempts to win you over. It would seem the art of attraction can sometimes be quid pro quo. Be that as it may, returning the favor can be a good thing.

You know you are doing something right when your potential love interest returns the favor via the art of attraction. The art of attraction is almost like doing favors for each other because his or her interest will only grow when your potential mate sees you are trying to please and thus win him or her over. It is very attractive to think about more than yourself when employing the art of attraction.

It is also very attractive to have and display some self-respect during the art of attraction. In short, don't go overboard with the art of attraction in trying to woo your potential love interest because he or she will see you don't really care for yourself but the other person so much that you end up compromising yourself in the process. Don't compromise who you are deep-down because you will only sell yourself short. Instead, show you have some self-respect by limiting things such as the number of drinks on a first date. In short, if your potential love interest sees you do have self-respect, he or she might be inclined to think you will also respect him or her as well.

In addition to respect via the art of attraction, also earned through repeated attempts to woo your potential love interest is trust. If your potential love interest trusts you and your attempts to attract him or her, that says a lot. It basically says I have confidence in you and entrust my innermost feelings, thoughts, and desires with you. Trust is clearly more than a word because when you have confidence and trust in the other party's attempts to attract you, you trust that they will not hurt you in any way. In short, you trust that your potential love interest has your best interests at heart.

Also at the heart of attraction is feeling both needed and wanted. Both men and women like to feel they are needed and wanted, so employ the art of attraction in such a way that the other party will end up feeling he or she can help you in some way. Perhaps let your potential love interest help you with a goal of yours like losing weight or being more social and outgoing. If you listen to your potential love interest's advice and tips, he or she will be inclined to believe you are taking very seriously what he or she has to say and offer. In short, your potential love interest will feel useful and needed.

Clearly, the art of attraction is a very delicate and nuanced thing. It takes time, trust, and careful attention to detail. Details like self-grooming and the setting can make a big difference in the attempt to woo your potential love interest. I know looks aren't everything, but it says a lot when you show up to a first date looking your best because that will imply some effort has gone into it. In other words, there's a fine line between self-acceptance and self-improvement.

The art of attraction is different for everybody. For example, I like a guy that can stimulate and move me with his wit and intelligence. I also like a guy that can take care of himself. Yet some ladies may prefer a guy who is nice and knows how to treat a lady. I think it all depends on what you are looking for at that moment. Are you looking for Mr. Right or Mr. Right Now? Clearly, the art of attraction can go in many directions with various outcomes.

Be that as it may, the art of attraction stays consistent throughout time. Women and men will always try to attract the other through time-proven techniques and methods. Fads might come and go, but thankfully the art of attraction does not. The art of attraction has much staying-power in comparison because the desire for human connection is stronger than any current and popular norm. The desire to attract and be attracted amid human connection in today's fast-paced Digital World is paramount in importance.

Chapter Summary

In this chapter, you have learned the art of attraction is both individualistic and universal. From the Law of Attraction to the color of your eyes and hair, the art of attraction is the hopeful appeal to your potential love interest that he or she will hopefully like you in return for your attempt to woo him or her. The attempt to be your best self to the attempt to improve some aspect of your potential love interest's life is not only attractive but appealing and downright sexy. In short, the art of attraction is:

- A mutual desire to be closer to your love interest.
- Liking the entire package of emotional, physical, and intellectual attributes.
- Both dynamic and interactive.
- The confidence to be your best self and to always improve.
- A reciprocal give-and-take of mutual interest in each other.
- Not controlling the outcome and letting it happen naturally.
- Doing favors for each other.
- Feeling both needed and wanted.
- Taking the time to earn one's trust and confidence with careful attention to detail.
- The human connection that results from your attempt to woo and attract.

There are also a few practical tasks that you can take action on to attract your potential love interest. These practical tasks will focus on what you can do right now to attract your love interest in your own life. For example, you can bathe daily to attract a potential love interest because cleanliness, as compared to the opposite, is attractive.

You can also practice flirting with a friend. In short, to attract a potential love interest, you can:

- Make personal hygiene a must.
- Practice flirting with a friend.
- Give compliments often.

In the next chapter, you will learn all about online dating and dating apps and websites like Tinder. You will learn what to look for and what to expect amid a world of sifting through online profiles and potential love interests. You will also learn what to do and what not to do when you are dating online. In short, dating online is an experience unto itself, and only the knowledgeable should even attempt it.

Chapter Five: Online Dating & Tinder: The Masterplan

Online dating can be confusing because there are so many options. It seems from the numerous amount of dating apps and websites to the copious amount of online potential love interests, the cornucopia of choices can be overwhelming. I'm here to help you make this transition to online dating a little easier with advice and tips to help you navigate the online dating world and succeed in your quest to find love.

Below, I have listed out tips that will help you find your match through online dating:

1. Be yourself: This is especially important when you are dating online because too many potential love interests lie in their online dating profile only to bag the girl, instead of showing who he or she really is in real life beyond the profile. Who you are in real life should be showcased online and not the other way around. Otherwise, disappointment may occur when you meet your potential love interest in real life

2. Don't wait too long to take the budding relationship offline: As soon as you are comfortable, perhaps have the online suitor call you or Skype so you can see if there is any organic chemistry. I say this because people are sometimes different when they are online as compared to their real everyday life offline. Online relationships are not the same as offline relationships given the lack of emotional connection between 2 laptops.

3. Don't be too revealing in your online profile: You still want to have something to talk about on your first meet/date beyond your online dating profile on Tinder. Although you do want to be yourself, don't give everything away in the first paragraph. Instead, describe who you are without going overboard with every little detail. Nobody wants to read five pages of your personal profile before seeing your picture. Be short, sweet, and concise without writing an essay.

4. Write about what you want in your potential love interest: Otherwise, you are just searching in the dark. What I mean is take the time to write a short paragraph about the similar attributes and characteristics you are looking for in a mate. This will pay off in the long run because you won't have to sift through a multitude of online dating profiles. Know thyself and your preferences for a potential love interest.

5. Upload a nice but not too professional picture of yourself: You don't want to look too uptight nor business-like in your personal profile picture because that might deter some potential suitors. What I'm saying is to look your best without appearing too polished. Your personal profile picture should showcase a softer more natural relaxed side of you as compared to the opposite. Also, be sure to upload more than one picture of yourself in various situations and/or settings because this will show who you are even more than compared to only one personal profile picture.

6. Make online conversations interesting and not dull: Make it interesting and your potential love interest will be more likely to respond in turn. Perhaps draw him or her in with a question or compliment about something in his or her online profile. For example, if the potential love interest enjoys wine-tastings, ask what his or her favorite type of wine is as a result of those tastings. It doesn't take this much thought to string together an interesting sentence and/or question.

7. Don't take the whole experience too seriously: Otherwise, your online dating experience won't be as much fun. So relax and enjoy it. In short, it's okay to meet new people for the sake of meeting them, as compared to the potential relationship always ending in a specific outcome. Just try to enjoy the light-hearted humor sometimes involved in meeting new people.

8. Don't become too disheartened by the whole experience: It will ultimately take time and patience to find Mr. Right For You. So if that means you have to sift through many online profiles and meet many duds, so be it. It will be worth it in the end when you do find him or her. Anything worthwhile takes repeated effort to make it happen.

9. Initiate the conversation: Don't be afraid to send out the first text message to your potential love interest. Otherwise, he or she might think you are not interested and move onto the next potential love interest. Guys like it when a woman shows she has integrity by taking action and making the first move. Too often women have been taught to be the complaisant recipient of courting instead of the initiators.

10. Have other methods of meeting people besides online: Don't make the Internet the only manner in which you are able to meet a potential love interest. That kind of limits your possibilities. It is good to have more than one route to meet people. The world will open up for you as you venture out to meet new people and potential love interests.

11. Step out of your comfort zone a bit: If you are used to doing things a certain way when it comes to online dating, perhaps try something a little different like taking the time to phone the person Or maybe branch out to try different dating apps till you figure out which one works best for you. That way you have more accessibility to more potential online love interests.

12. **Realize your worth:** In short, incline your potential online love interest to search you out instead of the other way around. What I mean is you are a treasure to be earned. If Mr. Right won't make the effort to come to you, then that suggests a lack of integrity and initiative on his or her part and has nothing to do with you personally. Realize your worth and move on.

13. **Don't give out too much personal information online:** Personal information on the first date like your home address or where you work is too private to share with somebody you just met. Instead, go to an agreed upon a public place with plenty of people around. you will ultimately feel safer than if you were alone with your potential love interest before really getting to know him or her. Don't end up a victim of some creepy stalker guy out there.

14. **Watch out for scam artists:** If your potential love interest's online dating profile sounds too good to be true, it probably is. Instead, cross-search his or her name with other social or dating apps to see if your potential love interest is already married or just looking to scam a pretty lady out of her money. It is invaluable to be diligent when checking out online dating profiles.

15. **Don't rush into anything:** I know that sounds contradictory in today's fast-paced Digital World, but it really is sound advice. I say that because if you rush into dating, especially online dating, you have a higher chance of getting hurt or taken advantage of. Nobody wants to be somebody else's romantic pawn, so take it easy and slow your roll.

16. **Don't critique or judge your online love interest:** In short, don't be so quick to critique your potential online love interest because of some little thing. You don't want to push away Mr. Right because of his unkempt goatee. Instead try to be more open-minded, because when we judge other people, that judgment could potentially be turned onto you like a revealing mirror. In short, when we critique others, we are usually critiquing some aspect of ourselves that we don't like to begin with.

17.   Find a potential love interest with similar concerns and goals in life: What I mean is if you both want to have children or if you both want to be healthier, by all means, go for it together. Yet if you and your potential love interest don't want the same things in life, it will be fairly hard to assimilate and acclimate to one another let alone be roomies and live together.

18.   Take the time to get to know your potential love interest: Before deciding if you really want to meet and hence date him or her offline, take the time to get to know your date online. Don't just ask two questions and then date. You should ask a lot of questions and get to know the individual's habits, turn-ons, quirks, likes, and dislikes, etc. If your idiosyncrasies mesh well, you may have won the jackpot of love!

19.   Be timely in your online dating responses: Don't wait too long to respond to your potential love interest if and when he or she sends you a personalized message. If you wait too long, you could risk losing the love of your life. In short, be timely in your online response to your potential love interest. In turn, he or she will hopefully respond to you expediently as well.

20.   Stand out amongst the herd through your online dating profile: There are millions of potential love interests with their common dating profiles. Don't follow the herd, but instead be one in a million by doing something different. If you are unique and one of a kind, you will indeed be a rare gem amongst many diamonds in the rough to your potential love interest.

21.   Use dating apps and matchmaking website like Tinder to your advantage: Online dating is not only educational but also advantageous to try to learn some online dating apps and websites out there like Tinder. Tinder is unique in that the dating app allows you to swipe right if you like a potential love interest's picture or swipe left if you don't in order to move onto the next online dating profile. In fact, there have been studies done on what makes some Tinder users more popular than others.

For example, one way some Tinder users are more noticeable than others is the color of their clothes that they choose to wear in their online dating profile picture, as compared to donning boring and lifeless neutrals. The brighter the clothes you wear on your online profile picture, the more they will make you stand out amongst a room full of wallflowers. In other words, don't be afraid to wear that red dress, especially if your skin tone agrees with it.

Another way popular Tinder users stand out is they smile in their online profile picture as compared to trying to look all sultry-like Brooke Shields. If you are trying too hard to look sultry, you may obtain the wrong kind of online suitors that may be after only one thing. Instead, a smile says more about you than if you pout, so why not enhance your mug with an upside-down frown and show those pearly whites?

Still, yet another way popular Tinder users set themselves apart from the crowd and get more swipes is if he or she doesn't hide from the camera. In short, try not to cover yourself up too much, because you won't get as many swipes to the right if potential online love interests cannot see you, to begin with. Showcasing your features says you have confidence and are not shy.

Popular Tinder users also look directly into the camera when a picture is taken for his or her online profile pic. Yet they don't stare down the camera either with a creepy intense gaze. So there is a fine line to knowing how to look directly into the camera for an online profile picture to be relevant. Try to relax your face and your eyes will follow suit and hence look more natural and inviting.

Yet another way popular Tinder users get more matches is if he or she uploads more than just a selfie. In short, selfies are so common today that they have worn themselves out of existence. Instead, try to upload pictures of yourself in different environments and settings with you in the foreground. Perhaps even post a full-body picture.

Popular Tinder users also stand out by beginning an exchange with their potential love interest with a gif. As long as the implied meaning is understood by both users, sending a *gif* is a great way to break the ice as compared to the typical standard text message of "hi." The gif could even be personalized with a picture of you in it, or perhaps personalize it to your potential love interests' likes or hobbies. For example, if your potential love interest likes skydiving, send him or her a gif with somebody skydiving.

Clearly exciting is when your potential love interest swipes right on Tinder because that means you have a possible romantic match! What you do from that point on is up to you, but now you have plenty of advice to help you navigate online dating apps and websites like Tinder. You have advice and tips from yesterday and today. Ironically enough, it seems while some dating advice stays consistent, other tips are more relevant to today's online culture of matchmaking.

The masterplan is to remember that some things never change when it comes to dating, but that change is necessary to date online. We can no longer rely on traditional methods of meeting a potential love interest because of the plethora of information in the Digital Age.

Everything about you is already online, making it more challenging to organically date because we feel like we already know the person when we do not in real life. It would seem an old-fashioned mortar and brick date no longer applies given virtual reality as well.

For example, instead of meeting in the cafe over a cup of coffee, you now meet in a virtual chat room to get to know each other. Another example is you decide whether you like somebody before organically meeting them via their online profile. Therefore it would seem the human connection is still necessary to see if there are real chemistry and attraction. In short, it is fairly hard to tell if somebody likes you if you can't read his or her body language. It would seem both dating and online dating require more than visuals but organic experiences.

It would seem organic dating experiences are enhanced by online dating apps and websites. They assist and aid us to locate and find potential love interests, as compared to the past when the dating pool was smaller and a lot more random. It seems online dating is more intentional these days than innocent because of how we can use the information gathered towards a person - either to help us or the opposite. Therefore, one's online reputation is paramount, especially when it comes to online dating.

Chapter Summary

In this chapter, you have learned that online dating is a whole new way to interact with a potential love interest in comparison to the years of yore. Be that as it may, some dating truths still apply to today's fast-paced Digital culture like manners and courtesy. In short, it would seem such dating turn-ons still resonate regardless of the time and age. However, in this chapter you have learned with regard to dating online:

- To be yourself when it comes to online dating.
- Don't wait too long to take the relationship offline.
- Don't reveal too much in your online dating profile.
- Write about what you want in a potential love interest.
- Upload a nice photo of yourself.
- Make your online conversation interesting and not dull.
- Don't take the online dating experience too seriously.
- Don't become disheartened.
- Initiate the conversation.
- Have other methods of meeting people besides online.
- Step out of your comfort zone via online dating.
- Realize your worth.
- Don't give out too much personal information online.
- Watch out for scam artists.
- Don't rush into it.
- Don't critique or judge your online love interest.
- Find a potential love interest with similar goals.
- Take the time to get to know your potential love interest.
- Be timely in your online dating responses.
- Stand out amongst the herd with your online profile.
- Use dating apps and matchmaking websites like Tinder to your advantage.

There are also a few practical tasks that you can take action on for online dating. These practical tasks will focus on what you can do right now to master online dating. For example, you can fill out an online profile at more than one dating app or matchmaking website to increase your experience with it and your chances of success. Another practical task you can undertake to master online dating is to like as many potential love interests as you can because this will drive the results you get for more similar online dating love interests. In short, you can:

- Fill out an online profile at more than one dating app or matchmaking website.
- Like as many love interests as you can drive results you get for similar online interests.
- Ask a friend for an objective opinion on your online dating profile.

In the next chapter, you will learn all about dating tips you need to know to succeed at dating and love both online and offline. These dating tips are important because they could affect the future of your potential love life. They could also potentially change your love life for the better. So ladies pay attention to the next chapter because we could all use a little help when it comes to wooing your potential love interest and keeping the relationship going.

Chapter Six: Dating Tips You Need To Know

Dating in the 21st century can be compared to a wine and painting class because sometimes you just don't know the full picture till you attempt to create it one tasteful color at a time. In the same vein, dating a potential love interest involves careful attention to detail. Details like your mood and your appearance will be noticed on a first date and possibly a second date. Therefore it is important to be mindful during a date but not to the point you overthink every little nuance and detail. After all, details are only part of the dating picture and not the resulting conclusion of those efforts.

Anything *'great'* takes effort and time. Likewise, dating requires the drive to create a lasting emotional connection and relationship with your potential love interest one get-together at a time through the intentional undertaking of useful first date tips. These useful first date tips will come in handy as you navigate and master the world of dating. Whether you are new or experienced to dating, there are dating tips that can be applied to almost every dating situation.

1. Be your authentic self: One reason is that a lot of us don't know how to successfully carry out the first date. Even married couples who go on date nights could use a little help. Help and advice like be yourself is priceless whether it's the first date or the hundredth date. Authenticity is key in a world of stereotypical romance wannabes. I'd rather date somebody who is comfortably genuine in comparison to dating the leader of the pack.

2. Take the lead during a date and initiate the conversation: This display of self-esteem in your abilities to not only be yourself but to woo your potential love interest sends a positive vibe. Your potential love interest will see you value yourself and know your worth through your actions to initiate not only the conversation but the potential future relationship as well. So ladies don't be afraid to take the reins on a first date.

3. Use your body language to infer interest: Moves like gently touching his arm or hand infers a genuine interest and signals your date to do the same in return. In short, reciprocal body language says a lot more than just words because even if you don't say much, your body language will speak volumes for you during a first date.

4. Know your limits on alcoholic drinks: If you are a lightweight, then don't consume seven shots in one sitting on your first date. It will be a turnoff to your potential love interest if you get sloppy drunk and can't even possess your own faculties. Besides, if you can't walk and talk during your first date, your potential love interest might end the date earlier than you want. In addition, you could be taken advantage of sexually.

5. Don't expect to be wined and dined: In short, consumption of food and drinks shouldn't be so paramount that you forget to focus on your date. The food should be good but not so over the top that your date thinks you are more concerned about being wined and dined than spending time with him or her. Be sure to fully engage your date and not just that glass of sparkling champagne. Enjoying in moderation suggests you do like to have fun but not go completely wild on a first date as well.

6. Wear classic clothing pieces: Include some classic clothing choices as compared to wild colors like a 1980s fluorescent-colored pair of high-tops. You want to look classy and polished, not like a novelty. Perhaps wear a casual but chic dress or even a nice pair of slacks with a cute top. Go casual but classy, as you don't want to appear like you are going to a job interview on your first date. In other words, it's okay to look more than nice but not too immaculately made-up like a Victorian doll.

7. Don't mention your ex: If you do, you will incline your date to feel you are not really paying attention to him or her. If you can't steer clear of referencing your ex during your first date, it is clear you are not ready for that first date. Perhaps seek help in working through your issues regarding your ex and get some closure before you even consider the first date with somebody new.

8. Put away your electronics: In short, abstain from your electronics during a first date and any date for that matter. I dare you to turn them off. Nothing says I'm ignoring you faster than a date scrolling on Facebook or checking his or her email. In fact, why not leave your electronics at home during your first date? That way you can fully engage your potential love interest.

9. Try and be playful and fun-loving: Your potential love interest on your first date will become more interested in you if you can show you are playful and fun-loving instead of going all serious on him or her. Maybe try being playful in lightheartedly teasing him or her a little instead of grilling your potential love interest with never-ending questions like some military authority. A fun-loving demeanor speaks volumes as to your character and can ease the tension on a first date.

10.   Don't turn your date into a research project before meeting him: One reason is that it goes without saying that the purpose of a first date and possibly a second date is to get to know him or her. If you do so much online research into your first date that you feel you already know him or her before you meet in real life, there is little point trying to spend time offline with the person. In short, don't ruin a potential first date by over-researching and thus jumping to conclusions about your date before you even know the person. First dates are supposed to be fun, not a research project.

11.   Leave your preconceived notions at the doorstep: This is because first dates are also supposed to be an organic learning experience, not only on what you are supposed to do but also about the other person. Instead, take the time to create and develop a bond that instills a healthy reciprocal interest and interaction between you two. Nobody wants to date somebody who tries to predict how the first date is going to go.

12.   Let him pay the bill if he chooses: Are you supposed to share the bill or let him pay for it in full? I'd say that is your personal preference, but men often like to show they are financially independent and successful. In short, if your date offers to pay the bill, don't argue and let him. You want your date to spend time with you because he or she likes you and enjoys your company, as compared to your potential love interest thinking he or she owes you something at the end of the first date.

13.   Be honest: This is because it would seem first dates are all about an exchange of thoughts, ideas, and feelings. When it comes to this interpersonal exchange, it is important to be honest about the whole thing. Otherwise, you could sabotage the chance of a future date and possibly the relationship. In short, be honest about who you are and what you really want. Don't lie to fit with what you think your potential love interest may want.

14.   Keep it short and sweet: I know it may seem counterintuitive because you want to take the time to get to know your potential love interest. Yet if there is little chemistry between you two, you will just be stuck spending time together and that's just uncomfortable, to say the least. In addition, you don't want to give everything away about yourself on their first date by spending a weekend with your potential love interest. Save some interaction for the second date and possible future.

15. **Put yourself in the right frame of mind before a first date:** For example, watch a silly movie or take a hot bubble bath or shower to calm the nerves. Maybe even have a glass of Moscato beforehand (don't get drunk). Whatever you have to do to relax, do it. That way by the time you get to your first date, you won't look all stressed and uptight.

16. **Burn off some of that nervous energy beforehand:** Perhaps you could go for a run or clean the house. By the time you are done expending that nervous energy, you will also be free from tension and anxiety and more ready for your first date. You will be more calm and confident as a result.

17. **Be mindful:** If you are mindful and conscientious about how your words and actions can affect other people like your first date, you will be more inclined to consider his or her feelings and reactions towards you as well. You will also be more inclined to listen to what your date has to say, as compared to worrying about whether he is looking at that girl in the red dress at the next table. In short, mindfully focus on yourself and your date.

18. **Give plenty of eye contact:** If you are too busy googling the waiter that just took your dinner order, that speaks volumes as to your level of interest in your date. It signals that you are not very interested at all in fact. To me, it would signal that you would rather be somewhere else and possibly with somebody else. This would only ruin the chance of any future dates with your potential love interest as well.

19. **Discuss what you are passionate about with your date:** Your potential love interest may enjoy it when you passionately discuss something that really matters to you like a cause you believe in or a hobby you are passionate about. I say this because when you become more animated about the topic of discussion, you pull in and attract your first date even more than if you just discussed the weather. In addition, the discovery of similar passions and hobbies might also be another reason to set up a second date as you attend that beading class together.

20.   **Have fun and pace yourself:** Take one step at a time to get to know your date and even yourself in the process. Also, keep the momentum and energy going. Have fun trying new things and getting to know one another. The point is to feel comfortable in your own skin whilst enjoying life to the max, so your date will be inclined to do the same.

Ironically first dating tips can apply to everyone, regardless of what your situation is. You can be married and go on date nights whilst getting to know one another again. You can also be a pro at dating and still need confidence to date your heart's desire. In short, first dating tips can help set the stage for a satisfying future relationship. The point is to keep the passion alive, whether dating or otherwise.

Chapter Summary

In this chapter, you have learned many first date tips and dating tips, in general, to help you succeed and master the world of dating. You have learned that the details of your first date are just as important as any momentous details of future dates and a possible relationship. You have also learned that dating isn't as hard as it seems if you just follow a few simple common sense tips. Dating can be fun if you:

- Are authentic and genuine.
- Take the lead and initiate conversation.
- Use your body language to infer interest.
- Know your limits on alcoholic drinks.
- Don't expect to be wined and dined.
- Wear classic clothing pieces.
- Don't mention your ex.
- Put away your electronics.
- Show you are playful and fun.
- Don't turn your date into a research project before you meet him.
- Leave your preconceived notions at the door.
- Let him pay the bill if he chooses.
- Are honest.
- Keep it short and sweet.
- Put yourself in the right frame of mind ahead of time.
- Burn off some of that nervous energy beforehand.
- Are Mindful.
- Give plenty of eye contact.
- Discuss what you're passionate about with your date.
- Have fun and pace yourself.

There are also a few practical tasks that you can take action on to engage in dating even more. These practical tasks will focus on what you can do right now to facilitate dating with grace and ease. For example, you can actually practice talking to your date in front of a mirror before the actual date. You could even group date with friends until you become more familiar with the person you are trying to date. In short, you can:

- Practice talking to your date in front of a mirror before the actual date..
- Go on a group date first.

- Sign up for a speed dating outing to get more experience with dating itself.

In the next chapter you will learn eight easy ways to maintain and improve your relationship, because let's face it, we could all use a little help there. Sometimes relationships get stuck in a rut and that is when we need to take action wholeheartedly and work on it. No relationship is perfect, and if it was, it would be boring. In short, expect the unexpected and you just might surprise yourself and your partner!

Chapter Seven: Eight Easy Ways To Maintain And Improve Your Relationship

Relationships are like crafts. You have to invest in it time after time to develop and create a beautiful masterpiece full of vitality and substance. Likewise, just like a beader has to acquire the beads for her craft, sometimes it helps when those in a relationship acquire relationship advice to build a healthier relationship full of energy and life. The fun is in choosing the what and the how to create this beautiful thing we call love. It is this careful attention to detail that allows a relationship to flourish and thrive.

If you devote your time and energy to your relationship, it becomes a lifeforce of its own that can sustain and nourish you both through anything. It will serve you both through the good times and the not so good times as your repeated efforts to nourish it will envelop and carry you both through life's ups and downs. Through marriage, kids, and work, you will ultimately have each other. This is a gift unto itself, and such a reward is to be treated with the utmost care.

It is this careful attention to details and each other that allows for growth within a relationship. If you really want a relationship to work for the both of you, you will put in the time and effort to make it happen. You might even step outside of your comfort zone to embrace a new skill to impress your love. Whatever the case may be, it is imperative to try your best.

Trying your best in a relationship means you pour your heart into your relationship wholeheartedly. It means you give it your all to make it work, and none of this holding back nonsense. It means you realize that as an adult, it is what you make it. The same goes for relationships too.

There should also be a natural ebb and flow to your relationship, a give and take that appeals to both parties, not just one. When you are in a relationship, you have to weigh the interests, concerns, and feelings of the other party in addition to your own. In short, relationships are like a balancing act you hope works out in the immediate future and in the long run.

Yet if you are always worried about the future of your relationship, it will be fairly challenging to focus on the love of your life. In short, you have to make the effort to be mindfully present and be at the moment with your love. In fact, both parties need to be mindfully present to make the relationship work. It is a conscientious effort from both love birds.

Having a relationship is kind of like having a relationship with yourself because sometimes you have to improve upon the status quo to be your best self to even take part in a relationship. Likewise, you want your relationship to be the best relationship possible. While it is okay to accept the relationship as it is, it is also okay to improve upon it as well. In short, try not to become too satisfied with the status-quo because you want to be able to expect the unexpected in your love life.

In this chapter, I will give you eight easy ways to maintain and improve your relationship with one tidbit at a time. Tidbits like loving yourself to being supportive will go a long way in maintaining the relationship you want. Once you maintain and improve upon the relationship you want, you both will be happier as a result. Time to take notes!

The first tidbit is to love yourself. Loving yourself is essential because when you fill your cup with love, you have it to give to others as well. You feel more near to your own heart, which allows you to have the heart to give to others you cherish. Loving yourself could include eating healthier intake and spend a little 'me-time' to buy yourself that sexy dress. In other words, you have to love and give to yourself before you can love and give to others.

Loving yourself could also mean you set limits on what you will accept from other people. In short, it's okay to say no if you don't like how you are being treated by somebody else. This also teaches your love, how to treat you in return, which will benefit the long-term relationship because you will have taught him or her how to love you.

It goes without saying that loving yourself is also allowing yourself to enjoy things. Giving yourself permission to enjoy things like a glass of wine or a new hobby loosens you up and frees your mind. As a result, you are more receptive and open to the love that others give you. When you are open and receptive to love, this creates a positive reaction in yourself and others which allows them to be open to love. After all, love reciprocates love.

Loving yourself is a full-time job sometimes. It is not a quick fix or a one-night affair that will solve all your problems either. It is a continual effort and dedication to nurture your whole self into the woman you know you are capable of becoming. After all, it is a natural instinct to take care of ourselves. It is also a natural instinct to not accept anything less.

It is not self-centered nor self-indulgent to love and to take care of yourself. After all, you are all you got at the end of the day sometimes. Instead, it is self-care and self-love. This compassion, understanding, and self-knowledge will allow you to flourish when all else fails. Even if the relationship doesn't work out, you still got you, which is plenty.

Loving yourself also means you are accepting of your flaws. If you can love your flaws and weaknesses as much as your perfections and strengths, that says you accept the entire package that is you. It also infers you have more than enough balance to love somebody else's. Nothing is more beautiful than pure self-acceptance of what makes you, you.

What also makes you-you is support from your loved one. Therefore, the second tidbit to maintaining and improving your relationship is to be supportive. If you are supportive of both yourself and the love of your life, this will flourish into a support system that can benefit both parties by encouraging each other to not only be yourselves but to be your best selves. In short, an ever-present support system encourages you to try.

Being supportive means you encourage each other to push forward in attempting to live your best life. In other words, it means you support each other by encouraging things such as physical, emotional, and mental growth. For example, you could gently motivate your partner to exercise more by doing it with him or her. Another example is you could persuasively incline your significant other to let go of something like a child leaving for college for the first time. Clearly, support means encouragement and growth in our lives, especially our love lives.

Support in our love lives could mean your loved one gaining the courage to try something new in the relationship like a date night. Encourage and gently persuade your loved one the benefits of date night by dressing up and wearing something sexy to the date. Perhaps even encourage him or her to flirt a little. Even the best of relationships need a date night every once in a while to revitalize the spark that initially brought you lovebirds together.

Being supportive could also mean just being there for the love of your life. In short, sometimes the biggest action we can undertake to support a loved one is to be present by his or her side. Whether this support is emotional or otherwise, it says a lot to the other party that you are with him or her, to begin with. Never underestimate nor take for granted that freely given support, because it is done with the utmost love and care.

Regardless of how you are supportive, it is imperative to let your loved one know you care from time to time. Otherwise, he or she may seek that support from elsewhere. Likewise, sometimes being supportive means an absence from your loved one in that too much support may enable an unhealthy relationship. It would seem supportive also includes healthy limits on what you will and will not tolerate in the relationship.

Being supportive also means not expecting anything in return as a result of that support. Support should be freely given and not with conditions. When you make support conditional, it only sends the opposite message, and that is what you don't want. Instead, give your time and encouragement without the promise of anything, and you will be rewarded when you see your loved one growing as a person.

Another way to show support is to be accepting of your loved one's friends and family. In short, the third tidbit to maintaining and improving your relationship is to be accepting of his friends and family and vice versa. When you are accepting of his friends and family, it shows you accept him or her as well. You could invite them over to hang out with your friends or you could go out as a group together to get to know each other. Either way, acceptance of each other's friends and family shows that you accept your loved one for who he or she is.

Acceptance of his friends and family could also imply you are serious about the relationship and ready to move forward because you are thinking about more than yourself at this point. You are also considering how his friends and family may feel about you, your friends, and family. And acceptance is key to any relationship, especially a romantic one. If you have trouble accepting your love's friends and family, you likewise have trouble accepting your love.

If you are accepting of his friends and family, it shows you can be a friend to your loved one. Being a friend will solidify the bond between you love birds even more than you both realize as friendship is just as important in the relationship. Case in point, many lasting relationships start off as friendships. Friendship is also important because his friends can help you know your loved one even more than they share information about past adventures with you.

Another benefit to accepting your love's friends and family is they will be more accepting of you, your friends, and your family. You might even have more friends and family to have fun and to be spontaneous with. And let's face it, spontaneity is also important in a romantic relationship. The relationship can become stagnant and ritualized otherwise. Therefore, it is important to take a step off the beaten path every now and again to try new things on a moment's notice. Your relationship will be invigorated as a result.

The fourth tidbit to maintaining and improving your relationship is spontaneity. Spontaneity can be fun because it is a naturally unconstrained impulse to do something uninhibited. This can give you something to look forward to instead of being stuck in a relationship rut. Shake things up every once in a while to see how it goes. Maybe surprise your love by taking him or her to a music concert or even an adventurous weekend will give your relationship the spark it needs to grow.

Spontaneity can give your relationship and romance new meaning as it brings it to life. In fact, pretend you are still dating him or her and consequently getting to know your love all over again. This will animate things between you two and bring you closer as you discover new ventures and each other as a result. It is okay to mix things up to bring you and your love out of a complaisant state of mind.

Spontaneity can also set the stage for the relationship to grow and flourish because both you and your love will be in the moment as opposed to otherwise. You will be more inclined to experience a spur-of-the-moment adventure with your love as you go with the flow. In other words, don't always plan everything. Relationships need more than careful planning to thrive.

Being spontaneous is like going on a roller coaster ride because you don't know exactly what is going to happen and when. You just go with the turns, flips, and loops to end up on your feet again. You enjoy the ride as the g-force overtakes you and begins to lift you out of your seat. Likewise, spontaneity has a force of its own as it can lift you out of a boring relationship routine.

Being spontaneous can also help in the bedroom because you surprise your love with new moves which can open the door to sexual spontaneity. In short, the fifth tidbit for maintaining and improving your relationship is to make time for hot sex. Don't get stuck in a sexual routine because the last thing you want is for things to get dull and consequently fizzle in the bedroom. Instead, liven things up by adding some romance to the setting.

Most people think that making time for hot sex means you wear something provocative like a teddy and high heels to encourage your love to join you in the bedroom. However, in reality, it could also mean you make extra time for each other at the end of the day by spending time being in proximity to your love. Maybe even playfully tease him or her. Maybe start with a little kiss and see where it goes.

I'm no Dr. Ruth, but the principles of lust should apply. Don't be afraid to enjoy a little bedroom action because it will ultimately bring you love birds closer together. It will allow you to connect in such a way that you both feel sexy and desired. In short, desire and pleasure are healthy to experience behind closed doors. Any healthy relationship needs to have a little desire to forge a healthy connection.

When you connect physically, emotionally, and mentally, the bond is as strong as ever between you and your love. It is the glue that holds you together through thick and thin. It is the force that unites and joins you together. In short, that special bond shared between you and your love is the stuff of relationships that stand the test of time. In other words, the sixth tidbit to maintaining and improving your relationship is to connect physically, emotionally, and mentally.

If you can connect physically, emotionally, and mentally, your relationship will be better off than if you just find one aspect to halfheartedly connect. Don't cheat yourself or your love out of this priceless human connection. What you want is the relationship to come full circle as you experience this connection simultaneously with your love. It is important to grow and develop as a couple, in part because it is about more than you now.

However, it is about you sometimes, especially as you learn to communicate to your loved one about what you really need and want from the relationship. Remembering to communicate is the seventh tidbit of advice to help you maintain and improve your relationship. How and when you communicate these things to your loved one is key. Do it with tact and grace, as compared to throwing a fit. Another piece of advice is to not wait till the end of the day when he is tired to bring it up.

There is a place and time for everything. Perhaps communicate to your loved one over dinner about you how really feel instead of putting it off because you are busy. If you do that, communication just becomes an occasional spurt of words interspersed with emotion. In short, communicate with each other regularly to avoid a ticking bomb of sorts. Regular communication will keep the doors open to your relationship as well and might just deflate any tension between you love birds.

Communication also allows you and your loved one to figure out if the relationship is heading in the right direction for both of you. If you don't communicate this through words, actions, and reactions, how can you expect to know what the next step is in a relationship? The future of the relationship might be in question if you can't even say sorry or more importantly, 'I love you.'

Clearly, words and even body language play a big part in two-way communication because they inform your loved one what the next step in the relationship should be and if everything between you two is okay, to begin with. Be honest and straightforward with your relationship communication, and it will do the same for you. In short, it is important to communicate as a team.

It is also important to work as a team within the relationship. Pointedly, the eighth tidbit of advice to maintaining and improving your relationship is to work as a team. Remember, it's not just about you anymore. It's now about you and your loved one together. Being a team means you work together to solve any problems if and as they arise. Working together also means you and your loved one do what you can to stay together.

Working as a team sometimes means you also put the other team member's needs before your own as you weigh your loved one needs and wants in addition to your own. It really is a system of checks and balances as you work it out to where both parties are satisfied and happy. For example, marriage is clearly about more than a piece of paper, it is about teamwork and love.

Teamwork is the dreamwork as they say. If you are only thinking about yourself in the relationship, it will be fairly hard to even have a healthy relationship to begin with because it will be unbalanced and out of proportion as one person centers it on his or her needs only. That is what you don't want. What you do want is your relationship to survive and thrive with balance, integrity, and love.

Chapter Summary

In this chapter, you have learned what it takes to maintain and improve your relationship. You have learned eight important tidbits of information that can help both you and your loved one survive and thrive. You have learned that attention to detail in a relationship is very important because it is this attention to detail that allows it to grow and flourish into something bigger than yourself. in short, you have learned that it is important to:

- Love yourself.
- Be supportive.
- Be accepting of his friends.
- Be spontaneous.

- Make time for hot sex.
- Connect physically, emotionally, and mentally.
- Communicate.
- Work together as a team.

There are also a few practical tasks that you can take action on to maintain and improve your relationship. These practical tasks will focus on what you can do right now to maintain and improve your own relationship with your loved one. For example, you can plan a mini vacation just for the two of you some weekend. You could even surprise your loved one with a priceless gift that means something more to him or her than a material possession. Perhaps donate your time to a cause your loved one believes in as a meaningful gift. In short, you can:

- Plan a mini vacation weekend for the two of you.
- Surprise your love with a meaningful gift.
- Make yourself available to offer your help or services if needed.

In the next chapter, you will learn seven common relationship challenges and how to fix them with grace. In short, these relationship challenges are not permanent if you take the time to do something about it now. Taking immediate action is key to making your relationship your best relationship for you and both your love. Anything is possible, including a healthy relationship.

Chapter Eight: Seven Common Relationship Challenges (And How To Fix Them)

Relationship problems are both unique and common. They are unique to the couple experiencing them but common because relationships are not perfect by any means. They are fraught with challenges and milestones. In addition, relationship problems are healthy to have because it suggests the relationship is growing and not staying stagnant. In short, relationship problems are a normal part of any relationship, but not the entire relationship itself.

Relationship problems are different for every couple given each partner's level of experience and personal maturity and development in the relationship. For example, while one partner may be more experienced with marriage, the other may be more experienced with personal autonomy. It is these unique differences that must somehow meld to create a functional and sustainable relationship. If both partners can compromise a little, perhaps a working solution can be reached until the next milestone of growth materializes.

Relationship problems or issues also stem from the fact that every individual is different in their genetics and the environment he or she grew up in. For example, one partner may have grown up an only child, while the other learned to live with numerous siblings during his or her wonder years. One partner may be more submissive and yielding while the other is more dominant and independent given his or her natural inherent characteristics and home environment. The point is these unique characteristics make for a romantic melting pot of sorts that somehow produces a fluid relationship.

Fluid relationships need the concurrent development of problems and their resulting solutions to grow and develop beyond the initial static presented by both parties in the relationship. That initial relationship static can create something beyond words if both parties in the relationship pay careful attention to its dynamics and characteristics. In short, don't let those characteristics determine the fate of the relationship and your love life.

Instead, use your relationship problems as an opportunity to grow and become even closer through trial and error. Perhaps see your money problems as an opportunity to learn more about each other. See what works and what doesn't in the attempt to solve the issue between you two. You have to try if you want the relationship to work.

In this chapter, you will learn seven common relationship challenges and how to fix them. Most couples experience these relationship challenges from time to time as the relationship follows a natural pattern or cycle. Since this cycle is always changing and evolving, it is important to be regularly consistent in your efforts to work on your relationship challenges. Consistency is key.

The first relationship challenge is trust. Trust is something you earn they say. However, trust can be loosely defined as an implied understanding between two people. This is an implied understanding of someone or something bigger than yourself. It suggests faith, confidence, and conviction in yours and the other person's abilities.

If you trust somebody to treat you right in a relationship, it implies you give the person the benefit of the doubt till proven otherwise. It also implies with certainty that things will pan out now and in the future between you love birds. Trust is bigger than you or me, yet it can also be so delicate a thing that sometimes it doesn't take much to break it. And when that happens, it can often be challenging to repair. It would seem trust takes on a life of its own as it envelopes the actions and words of more than one person.

One the other hand, if somebody trusts you, it implies he or she likewise has faith and confidence in your ability to treat him or her right with assurance. It also simultaneously implies that you won't hurt or damage your partner or the relationship in any shape or form. Believe me when I say trust is a big concept to not only define but to carry out and perform day to day. It would seem trust is an action bigger than words. If you and your partner are in a long-standing relationship, he or she trusts that you indeed have his or her best interests at heart.

Trust is the glue that holds the relationship together. In short, everything in the relationship that matters comes down to trusting yourself and your partner. If you have a challenging time trusting your partner for whatever reason, this could infer the level of trust between you two is not what it once was at the beginning of the romantic relationship. In such a case, here are some tips to help you regain that priceless trust back.

Tip number one to earning and keeping his or her trust is to have a conversation to get to the heart of the issue that decreased his or her trust in you to begin with. That way you are both on the same page about it. It is important to listen to what the other person has to say because perhaps just doing so will start the recovery process to trust you again. Trust builds upon trust.

Tip number two to earning his or her trust is to take action. Whether you've lost your partner's trust or vice versa, taking action after the talk is just as important. This is an action that will hopefully earn his or her trust in you again (or vice versa). Actions to reconstitute trust involve things like being there for him or her and even showing you are worthy and capable of the trust that initially bonded you love birds together.

Tip number three to earning his or her trust is to define what it means to you through your own words and actions to demonstrate to your partner. If you can show your partner that you understand what trust is, perhaps he or she will eventually come around through repeated efforts to define it. Like I mentioned previously, trust build upon trust. It would seem the word is no match for the action it entails.

Speaking of taking action, the second relationship challenge is to make the relationship a top priority. This can often be challenging with all the responsibilities we undertake to maintain and develop the relationship itself. Responsibilities like work and kids take time as well and can often be draining. Be that as it may, if you take the time to prioritize your relationship, you might instead feel energized from the attempt. Perhaps at the end of every day, spend a little time snuggling and catching up.

Your partner will end up feeling needed and wanted as you make him or her a top priority in your life through your actions, instead of allowing the relationship to fall by the wayside. In addition, perhaps this gesture will be returned making the relationship more important than the television or cellphone. When you make time for each other, the benefits of doing so are numerous and plenty. Putting value into your love and hence the relationship will pay it forward for years to come.

Clearly, it is important to make time in your schedule to spend time together. Maybe even arrange an outing with your love. Take your partner to his or her favorite restaurant. Another suggestion to incline your partner to feel important and valued as a top priority is to sign up for a class together on his or her favorite hobby. This move will incline your partner to feel very valued as you engage in his or her favorite passion with them.

Be that as it may, sometimes you have to make yourself a priority to make your love and the relationship top seniority in your life. In short, taking care of yourself will ultimately take care of the relationship in some way if you can also give to yourself as well. Doing little things for yourself like going for a nature walk outside will do wonders for your relationship because you will ultimately feel more worthwhile. Sometimes you have to value yourself before you can value others to make them a top priority.

Prioritizing your relationship infers there is more communication than previously because you and your partner have clearly taken the time to value one another and as a result, there is hopefully more interaction between you love birds. In short, the third relationship challenge is communication. Communication with your words and actions is important because it infers how you truly think and feel, especially in regards to the love of your life. If you don't communicate, it will be fairly challenging to have a relationship to begin with.

Communication between couples is very important because it keeps the door open for the exchange of our innermost thoughts, feelings, and ideas with one another. It is like an interactive transmission of messages and signals that allows us to understand and learn from each other through words, reactions, and body language. It is this transfer of expression that allows us to grow and develop both individually and as a group, albeit a couple. Case in point is when you've been with somebody for so long, that he or she can read and understand you before you even know what's internally going on with yourself.

It would seem communication can be both internal and external in that internal communication includes our innermost thoughts and feelings while external communication includes our actions and reactions to those thoughts and feelings from ourselves and from others. It would seem this kind of communication is more a feedback loop in which we try to understand both the input and the output of emotion and thoughts. It is this constant flow that feeds on itself. In short, emotion feeds an emotion, and thoughts lead to other thoughts.

However, when there is a lack of communication, a person will eventually withdraw from others and even from himself or herself. This is when emotions and thoughts become out of proportion and distorted. In short, sometimes we need others to ground us in what we're feeling and thinking through their communicative attempts to understand what is going on with us. Communication is key to a relationship, even with ourselves.

Likewise, a couple needs to communicate with each other to keep the relationship open and fluid. If either party in the relationship withdraws from the other for whatever reason, the relationship suffers. Things become unbalanced and the relationship eventually slows to a standstill like a feedback loop stalling for lack of input and even output. In short, couples that communicate keep their relationship active and dynamic. They also keep the relationship alive.

One way to keep the relationship alive and to fix a lack of communication within it is to make time to be with your partner. It is fairly challenging to communicate if you aren't even together to begin with. Maybe do an activity you both enjoy. Perhaps going for a walk will free up your minds enough through physical activity that somebody begins the conversation. Talking is only the beginning of opening the doors of communication between both you and your partner. Once that door is open, communication becomes more natural and relaxed.

A second way to fix a lack of communication between you and your partner is to do something nice for your partner because that will incline him or her to respond to you, perhaps with a smile of gratification. Showing and expressing gratification often opens the door to conversation because the quality of life improves by simply saying "thank you." These words are so simple, yet they open so many doors, especially to communication.

A third way to fix a lack of communication is to incline your partner to use his or her body language more to signal to you how he or she is really feeling. In other words, body language can often speak louder than words. Even so, it is important to use and employ wisely, because you don't want to overdo it. In the same vein, it is also important to do naturally in response to your partner. I know I'm fairly easy to read through my facial expressions.

Freedom of expression is important in any relationship. Whether that expression is emotional or physical, it is invaluable in showing your partner how you feel (within reason). The fourth relationship challenge is making time for sex. This can be hard to do when you become so busy, that you are just exhausted at the end of the day because the energy just isn't there after working 10 hours. If this is the case, perhaps try a romantic weekend getaway for the two of you.

Sex is important because it releases hormones and endorphins that make us feel good and feel good about each other. Sex bonds you two even closer together given the chemical, physiological, and emotional reactions intimately shared during a romantic rendezvous. Sex is also something to look forward to in the relationship. If you don't make time for sexual encounters between you and your loved one, you do yourself a disservice. In short, you can lose your motivation and drive for other things as well cause that energy just won't be there.

One easy way to make time for sex is to sneak it in at a moment's notice when you can. Whether it's early morning or late afternoon, little sexy gestures to your partner will clue him or her to want to rendezvous with you. Maybe even sexting each other beforehand will inflame your desire and motivate you to meet him or her somewhere. Either way, the alluring promise of sex will have you anticipating something mutually pleasurable in the relationship.

A second way to make time for sex is to call and ask the babysitter to watch the kids while you and your love hook up. You don't even have to go anywhere if the babysitter takes the kids out for a few hours. In short, sometimes staying home to engage in sex can be just as exciting when both of you make the effort to satisfy your desires. Maybe even take a shower together to spark the encounter.

Yet meeting somewhere outside the home like a fancy hotel room can be expensive. In fact, money woes themselves can sometimes sabotage that desire for fulfillment. In short, the fifth relationship challenge is money. From how to save it to how to spend it, money problems can derail a loving relationship if they are not managed with care. In other words, you are just asking for trouble if you are not honest and forthcoming with your partner about money. The last thing you want is for the love of your life to leave you because you got greedy with credit cards.

Money can clearly be the root of relationship problems, especially if one partner makes more than the other because it is possible the partner who makes less money might feel inferior somehow compared to the partner that brings home the bread. Be that as it may, the money should be divvied up so that each partner has his or her financial responsibilities in the relationship according to who makes what. And even if only one partner makes the money, there should still be some allocated to the one who doesn't because it implies a responsible allocation of financial resources between both parties.

One way to solve money problems is to take the time to go to a finance expert with all your expenses, debt, and savings, to get the help you need to be financially stable as a couple. In short, sometimes you have to put it on the table to see what you are working with and go from there. Perhaps make a list if necessary expenses to see what you need in comparison to what you want. One thing I do is to keep all my bills in a ledger with their respective dates to be paid. That way I can keep track of my finances better than if I just paid my bills on the fly.

A second way to solve money problems is to simply not spend it. If you are an impulsive shopper, don't go to eBay after a few glasses of wine. In short, don't drink and shop. Instead, try to develop other satisfying habits instead of spending money. Perhaps save a little each month for unexpected expenses, so that way you are covered just in case one should materialize at a moment's notice. The couple that saves together stays together.

If you stay together with your significant other, it is likely there are everyday chores that need to be done. Chores like doing the dishes to taking out the garbage. Let's face it, very few of us enjoy doing them. Be that as it may, sometimes you have to be an adult and do things you don't want to do. In other words, the sixth relationship challenge is doing the chores at home.

Doing chores at home can be problematic for any couple given stereotypical gender roles. In short, a lot of women assume if the man is the breadwinner, the woman should pull her weight in doing the chores. However, there is nothing sexier than a man doing the dishes.

In short, couples should work together to complete daily chores and errands. One benefit or working together as a couple to completing daily chores and errands is that you get to spend more time with your love and consequently get to know him or her better.

Another way to solving the relationship challenge of doing chores at home in addition to cleaning together is to pace yourself as a couple in doing them. Don't try to do them all in one day, because you will burn yourself out in the process, and chore-burnout isn't good for any couple. The last thing you want as a couple is for the house to be sloppy messy. At some point, you might even be too tired to care about chores at the moment. Instead, set realistic goals for chores you can actually do, as compared to going all Super Woman on them.

Every cleaning Super Hero must deal with conflict because cleaning is a never-ending job that constantly reinvents itself given the fact that life is naturally messy. Be that as it may, conflict is a natural part of life and of any relationship because the presence of it implies development and growth. In addition, not every couple is going to get along all the time. Conflict is natural and necessary for partners to develop as a long-standing couple. The seventh relationship challenge is clearly conflict.

It is how you deal with conflict individually and as a couple that matters. If you get angry at every little thing your partner does instead of simply talking to him or her about it, you have not successfully dealt with conflict. How we deal with conflict individually also affects how we deal with conflict as a couple because various conflict management styles naturally lend themselves to others. What I mean is if you're accommodating your partner's needs before your own in a conflict, you just might be avoiding the conflict altogether by taking yourself out of the equation. In other words, loving partners in a relationship won't survive if they take themselves out of the equation.

Yet conflict can be a good thing as it teaches you to solve problems together, especially problems in a relationship. The experience can bring you closer together as you learn to let the smaller things go. In other words, conflict management is key to relationship survival as you learn to work it out both individually and as a couple.

One way to mediate conflict in a relationship is to find a common middle ground that satisfies both parties. This could even deflate the conflict a bit itself given both parties feel their needs and wants have been at least considered. If both partners' needs have been considered on common ground, they will also have less to disagree about. Instead, they might even collaborate and work together to solve the issue. So much for conflict.

Another way to handle conflict in a relationship is to acknowledge it and move on. Sometimes simply acknowledging the conflict can do wonders because the action implies to your partner that you hear what he or she is trying to say as compared to ignoring it. Once you acknowledge the problem, you can begin to deconstruct it to understand it better from more than one perspective. Sometimes putting yourself in another's shoes to open your eyes as to how he or she deals with things can bring resolution.

Chapter Summary

Clearly, the resolution to the seven common relationship challenges of trust, making the relationship a top priority, communication, time for sex, money woes, chores at home, and conflict can bring a couple closer together through trial and error. It is this process that allows for the development and growth of the couple because they learn the most successful method of resolution to their problems and challenges. If the couple can work together, they can indeed live, laugh, and love together. Just remember to:

- Talk.
- Take Action.
- Make time for each other.
- Have lots of good sex!
- Be honest about money.
- Do chores together.
- Work on conflict resolution.

There are also a few practical tasks that you can take action on to fix relationship challenges. These practical tasks will focus on what you can do right now to fix your personal relationship challenges. For example, you can actively listen to what your partner is saying and expressing. You could also ask for clarification as to what your partner is expressing. In short, you can:

- Actively listen.
- Ask for clarification.
- Repeat back to your partner what he or she has expressed to you.

In the next chapter, you will learn how to date and actually enjoy it. Dating should be fun for both parties as they learn about what makes each other tick. If you know what to do, that's half the battle. So sit back and enjoy the ride!

Chapter Nine: How To Date And Actually Enjoy It

Too often people look at dating like a competitive sport. This mindset of win or lose is all wrong when it comes to dating because it suggests dating is a game in which one most score. Yet even the players can't always out-think and outmaneuver the other. In addition, dating is more cooperative and collaborative whereas sports are more competitive and cutthroat. It would seem in a culture of competition, dating goes against the norm.

Be that as it may, dating and sports are similar in that people go into it expecting a successful outcome. They expect to bring home the prize. Whether that reward is a gold medal or your potential love interest, it usually takes repeated efforts to earn it. Yet repeated effort and incentive are needed to even participate sometimes.

It all comes down to your strategy. In other words, how you play the game is just as important as whether you achieve success. If you play the game to win, you will ultimately lose more than you bargained for. Yet if you play the game just to play the game, you ultimately win more than you think. Sometimes just being present to even play is the reward.

The intent to have fun should be your ultimate goal when you go out on a date as compared to expecting to get something out of it. In short, dating can be fun if you have the right mindset and outlook. Sometimes games and even dating can be fun if you don't take the whole thing too seriously. However, don't be a spectator and sit on the sidelines either. Instead, just show up to see what happens.

What you don't want to do is date like you're competing in some sports arena because even Spartacus gets tired after a while from giving it his all. Likewise, if you suffer from dating burnout, perhaps take a break and take care of yourself first. Maybe even change the setting to something more of a level playing field for both of you. And remember to pace yourself and save some energy for the next date and maybe even the future relationship.

Pacing yourself during a date means you take your time with the whole experience as you get to know your love interest as compared to rushing into it like a football player with all your gear or armor on. In short, sustained enthusiasm and liveliness will hopefully produce better results when dating rather than intense short bursts of energy. However, energy is vital during your date because you are learning about him or her.

In fact, the process of learning and dating are quite similar in that you must pay attention to understand the subject-your date. Your date can give you all the information you need to determine whether there is a mutual interest between you two. Information like body language will help you perceive whether to go on a second date. It is like a student-teacher scenario because while one party is throwing out the signals, the other is soaking it up. It is this give-and-take that instructs both parties how and whether to respond to the other.

In addition to paying attention on a date, your memory can also come in handy as you receive, store, use, and retrieve the information given to you by your date and the entire experience. For example, if your date keeps blushing in response to your attempts to flirt, that information can be used to infer he or she likes you. You eventually figure out what works and what doesn't work on a date as you apply that memory to the second date.

Another active process of learning that comes in handy on a date beside paying attention and memory is language. Language whether spoken or unspoken is useful on a date because it allows either party to give, express, and receive information about the other and the status of the date itself. Language is so effective that it can communicate things such as whether to ask for a hug or kiss. Clearly, the process of learning on a date never stops, even after you commit to each other for the long term. It is continual like the seasons.

Yet how to date and enjoy it are not as straightforward and defined as learning and sports. It is less defined and more ambiguous because everyone is different when it comes to dating and it's enjoyment. Some people like a formal date with a fancy dinner where others like an informal date with a walk on a nature trail somewhere. In fact, some people don't enjoy dating at all no matter what you do or where you go.

It is these naysayers that can ruin the dating experience for everyone else as they try to put archaic definitions and rules on what a worthy date is instead of just letting it be and unfold naturally. One reason naysayers may not like dating is that they can't control everything that happens during a date, feelings, and consequently love. Dating, feelings, and love are like uncontrollable forces of nature that have lives of their own in part because they are more unpredictable. Be that as it may, dating can be fun if you just relax and let go of what you think it's supposed to be. There is no script for how it is supposed to go.

In the same vein, the human connection can sometimes be unpredictable because people differ in their motives, needs, and wants. One person may want to hook up sexually while another may want a more long-term relationship. Whatever the case may be, our senses awaken and deepen through contact with another person. In short, sight, sound, smell, taste, and touch are more fun if they are ultimately shared and experienced together. It is this shared experience during a date that is enjoyable.

Also enjoyable and funny sometimes is human nature in relation to the human connection during a date. In other words, sometimes we might fumble when we try to physically, emotionally, and mentally connect, and that's okay. If you happen to trip while attempting to walk all sexy in a pair of high heels, it is okay to laugh at yourself. It would seem humor is an essential ingredient to a first date especially when you are trying to get to know each other. If you can laugh both at yourself and your potential love interest at your attempts at the human social connection, you got a winner.

You can also enjoy a date more by learning a new hobby or skill together. Perhaps try your hand at making gourmet food or a new way to dance. By being in proximity to one another, you will have a higher chance of inadvertently coming into contact with your potential love interest. This will be an enjoyable and fun way to flirt and get to know one another. So don't be afraid to dance the night away!

You might also enjoy dates more if you went out on more of them. Socializing more might incline you to feel less awkward and more confident also as your social circle gets bigger as a result. In short, your enjoyment of people will increase given you will make more friends and acquire more experience just being around other people. This will help you relax more and be your genuine self in the company of others.

Another way to enjoy dates is to date with other couples also going out on a date. This will increase your social interaction and as a result, incline you to feel more outgoing. The more outgoing you are, the more friends you will ultimately attract and the more people will want to be around you. Confident attracts confidence.

Enjoying a date will also be easier if you are less judgemental of every little thing during the date. For example, if you find fault with the dive he took you for cheeseburgers and fries, maybe you are mirroring your own self-judgment. When you find fault in yourself and in the quality of every little detail and nuance, you will be miserable. Instead, be more accepting of the status quo and you might just be surprised.

Having fun on a date will also be more likely to occur when you say *'please', 'thank you', and 'you're welcome'*. Being courteous with these words implies you are well-mannered and as a result can be charming, considerate, and gracious during a date. It will also allow for more pleasant interaction to occur because your date will see you can be delightful with how you express and give gratitude. Yet don't go overboard in that expression either because it could imply you are likewise being condescending and that is what you don't want during a date when you are first getting to know somebody.

Another secret to enjoying a date is to be true to your innermost identity as opposed to feigning another one because you think it will make you more attractive to your date. Your date will eventually see through the charade when he calls you on your claim to be an expert skydiver as you scream on the way down, anyway. In short, you have to naturally be *'you'* according to your character and instincts. Being yourself is ultimately more fun anyhow.

Enjoying a date is quite possible if you don't have too many unrealistic expectations. In short, unrealistic standards will only disappoint and displease yourself and even your date. It might even incline him or her to feel inadequate somehow as they pick up on missing the mark to please you. That is what you don't want when you are trying to become familiar with the whole dating process and your potential love interest. Instead, be happy and grateful for the date itself.

Still, yet another way to enjoying a date is to let your hair down. Allow yourself to behave freely with your date in comparison to putting restrictions on what you can and cannot do. Instead, this freedom of expression between you two will ultimately let you and your date perceive if there is free-flowing natural chemistry, to begin with as opposed to just going through the motions.

Dating can be fun and enjoyable if you view it like you're going to an amusement park of sorts. You are there to try the rides, games, and food as you discover what you like and don't like. For example, some people like the intensity of a thrilling roller-coaster while others prefer the more subdued experience that you get from a carousel. Either way, the point is you have fun and enjoy yourself.

Having fun and enjoying yourself during a date is more suggestible than acting like your date is the new car model that you take out on a test drive for future purchase. Going for a test drive with your new model implies you are trying to manipulate the controls and where you end up with your date. This is unlike the process and experience of dating because you can't always steer into the direction of the date. Sometimes you have to sit and wait to see which signal you get next.

When you are more receptive to the signals your date sends to you, you ultimately have more fun during the date. This is because you are more open to new ideas and suggestions as compared to staying in the predictable comfort zone of stereotypical dating. In fact, dating is like stepping outside your comfort zone because sometimes you must proactively try new things to make a connection with your potential love interest as compared to reflexively reacting like an amoeba.

However, since fun dating is interactive, it requires more than one person or cell. It requires two people interacting to attract one another. Fun dating all comes down to Newton's third law of motion which basically implies for every action and reaction, motion materializes. And if your potential love interest moves you through his or her flirty ways, he or she has evoked something akin to an emotive movement within you like a smile or laughter. It is this smile or laughter that suggests he or she is indeed having fun.

Fun describes recreational entertainment which creates a pleasant experience. In the grammatical sense, it is an abstract noun or thing which suggests a state or condition with no physical reality that can be touched or seen with the senses. It simply is. However, the word enjoying is a verb that suggests a more active mode of being in which the senses must be involved somehow. Therefore, if you are enjoying your date, you are indeed actively present in every sense of the word.

As with anything else in life, dating all comes down to perspective and your point of view. If you view dating as a chore on a to-do list, you won't have very much fun and neither will your date. Yet if you view dating as the opportunity to enjoy and learn something new and fun, you might just surprise yourself as you creatively reach for that human connection. After all, fun dating is about connecting with people as imaginatively as you can.

The more imaginative you are on a date, the more fun it will be. In addition, you will be remembered and stand out more to your date if you are innovative and original in your attempts to have fun. Perhaps invent a new way to try something new like food. Maybe instead of the typical dinner and drinks, you could go on a culinary adventure by going to the local grocery store on the sample day. One time my husband and I did this, and we enjoyed ourselves as we tried various tidbits of Italian food, Chinese Food, and even some fancy apple liquor.

Dating can clearly be fun if you make it a memorable experience for both you and your date. Make the date notably unforgettable by adding new and different twists and turns to surprise your potential love interest. In short, it is beneficial to think and act outside the box on your date to make an impression, albeit one worth remembering.

Chapter Summary

In this chapter, you have learned how to date and actually enjoy it. You have learned that perspective is key to an enjoyable date, as well as more specific actions you can undertake to have fun during your date. You have also learned that having fun and enjoying the dating process and experience is what you make it as opposed to letting the date passively happen. In order to avoid this idle acquiescence of the dating process, you can:

- Mindfully be at the moment.
- Pace yourself.
- Pay attention.
- Expect the unexpected.
- Use your five senses.
- Don't take it so seriously.
- Learn and experience a new skill or hobby together.
- Go out on more dates.
- Go out on dates with other couples.
- Be less judgemental.
- Have manners.
- Be yourself.
- Don't have an unrealistic expectation.
- Let your hair down and have fun.

- Be receptive to new ideas and suggestions.
- Be imaginative and original.

There are also a few practical tasks that you can take action on to enjoy your date. These practical tasks will focus on what you can do right now to improve the dating experience whilst also enjoying it. For example, you can say or do something silly to loosen the tension like tell a joke or story. You could even enact small gestures of kindness like opening a door for your date. In short, you can:

- Say or do something to break the ice.
- Enact small gestures of kindness like opening the door for your date.
- Genuinely smile and laugh on a date.

In the next chapter, you will learn how to stay safe whilst online dating. In short, you will learn what to do and what not to do while you are considering going out on a first date with your potential love interest after checking out his or her online dating profile, in addition to managing your own.

Chapter Ten: How To Stay Safe Whilst Online Dating

Offline organic dating and online dating are similar in that you want the experience to be fun, enjoyable, and safe. You want to be able to have a pleasant experience whilst feeling secure that nothing problematic is going to occur. Yet with all the technological advances in today's world that allow us to live a better quality life, it would seem the information overload puts us in a precarious position putting your personal safety and security at risk. The last thing you want is to feel you are in danger because your personal details are all over social media websites and dating apps. Sometimes your online personal and private details like where you work are at risk given things like privacy settings.

Be that as it may, online dating requires vigilance and awareness to ensure you and your personal information are indeed safe and secure. It requires you to not only be more aware of your physical surroundings and location but also in the online setting. In short, you can feel just as vulnerable when your personal information is readily available to any joe. The last thing you want is to feel your safety is compromised because you put your home address on that dating app. It would seem online safety is synonymous with personal safety.

Personal safety and welfare begin with awareness. Awareness is the ability to have a cognizant perception of something. Something like how your actions affect others' actions. Likewise, self-awareness is the awareness of yourself in relation to something like your environment. And you definitely want to be self-aware in today's Information Age.

Self-awareness in the Information Age requires you take note of your actions because even your friends will post stuff about you online. In short, self-awareness requires you to be aware of both your actions and reputation both online and offline. In fact, what you do offline affects what you do online and vice versa. On that note, online dating involves the action of swiping right on a dating app like Tinder to perpetuate the offline action of an organic date to begin with.

Online dating takes self-awareness to do it right. You want to let people know who you are without giving too much personal and private information away. In other words, while you want to share details like your favorite color or vacation spot, you don't want to give away your private phone number. In short, there is a difference between sharing personal details that define who you are and giving away too much personal and private information that compromises your personal well-being. In other words, you want to protect yourself from people like scam artists and predators that might take advantage of you and your personal information.

Protecting your personal information is a must if you want to be safe online and offline. Doing so ensures you won't be a victim of a crime like identity theft or even worse. Clearly, it is beneficial to protect your online personal identity. It is also beneficial to protect your online identity because you also acquire or get possession of other things like a Netflix account or a potential love interest.

A potential love interest will gain knowledge of your online personal details and information when he or she views your online dating profile. This knowledge will be used to determine if he or she is interested in you and if he or she wants to go on a date with you. However, this knowledge can also be used to group you together with other similar online dating profiles as well, so your potential love interest will view more personal information in addition to your own online dating profile. How you characterize your online personal dating profile is key to gaining your potential love interest's attention and your well-being and safety.

Safety and well-being online and consequently offline during a date means that you don't color your online dating profile with sexually suggestive words or pictures. Doing so might attract the wrong kind of person, and that is what you don't want. Instead, what you do want to do to be safe regarding your online dating profile is to be less suggestive and more neutral with your personal details. It is okay to be intricately thorough without being provocative.

In addition, your online dating profile should not contain any personal information that pinpoints your whereabouts or locations you frequent. In other words, even if an online dating app or website requests your work or home information as part of your dating profile, don't give it because then some perp pretending to be interested in you could track you down when you least expect it. In addition, don't reveal your personal phone number because a stranger could Google it and do a reverse phone lookup, in effect discovering your location that way as well. Even Facebook has a feature called 'Friends Nearby,' where you can see who is in the same vicinity. Nobody wants a random weirdo to track them down.

On the other hand, it might be okay to reveal your location to friends and family when you are on a date resulting from meeting somebody from a matchmaking app or website. In other words, when you are meeting somebody for the first time, it is okay to let your friends and family know where you are and for how long. That way they can check up on you during or after the initial date. It's better to be safe than sorry.

Another way to be safe whilst dating online is to not have your potential love interest pick you up at your house or take you home after the date. In addition to organizing your transportation to and from the date, wait until you know him or her better before even inviting them to your house as well. The last thing you want is some stranger knowing where you live.

It also goes without saying that the first time you meet somebody new from dating online, you should hook up at a public place for personal safety reasons. You could meet at a coffee shop, a cafe, or even a mini-golf course. What you don't want to do is end up alone with this new person because you don't really know him or her from Jack or Joe. The more people around, the better.

Another way to be safe dating online and just plain dating is to carry a self-defense weapon of some kind like pepper spray or a mini safety air horn. These might come in handy if your date tries to pull anything sketchy and untoward. When you're meeting somebody for the first time on a date, you don't want to leave your personal well-being and safety to chance.

Dating online requires a certain level of self-vigilance when you're in an unfamiliar situation or environment as a result. For example, if you and your date go to a new local bar, do not leave your drink unattended. In short, there are all sorts of things to detect drinks spiked with date rape drugs. For example, nail polish and even straws do this. It would not be good to wake up the next morning and not remember events the night before.

In addition to watching your drink while out on a date with the potential love interest you've just met online, it is also important to remember to not indulge in alcoholic drinks too much. It is okay to have one or two to relax the nerves, but don't get so drunk that you end putting yourself in a compromising situation. Know your limits.

It is also important to scrutinize and review your date's online dating profile against his or her social media profiles so you can see if your date is who he or she claims to be in real life. In short, if it sounds too good to be true online with regard to your potential love interest, it probably is. On that note, watch out for fake Facebook profiles as well.

In addition, your online dating profile or your social media profiles should not include your entire name because you will be easier to look up and Google. In short, somebody can learn more private information about you this way. Instead, maybe just use your first name in your online profiles to avoid meeting a random weirdo.

If you do decide to date somebody after checking out his or her online dating profile, maybe ask your friends if they know the person. If they do, they will already have information as to what kind of person your date is in real life. In short, procure the help of your friends to ascertain the character of your date before you even go on the date.

Before you go on the first date, be sure to employ the online dating app's messaging feature instead of calling him or her directly from your cell phone. This will protect you in that your potential love interest won't get your private cell number and call you all day every day. The last thing you want when things go sour is to get harassed by somebody you just met. That would unnerve me just a tad.

Although online dating requires a level of self-vigilance, it is also wise to go somewhere where security cameras are also present. That way if something were to happen, it will be caught on camera, and can be used to benefit your safety and well-being. In short, footage of your date might prove invaluable, especially with a sketchy character.

It seems online dating can be fraught with many uncertainties. Uncertainties like your personal safety and well-being come into play given the plethora of personal and private information online for all eyes to see. It is this exposure of personal, private information itself that can feel like a data breach of sorts. You end up feeling compromised one way, or another which is why we got to take our personal security so seriously. It would seem online dating is no exception.

In fact, online dating seems to amplify your personal vulnerability in a number of ways from the validity and authenticity of who you meet during a date to the safekeeping and preservation of your personal information. Be that as it may, another way to protect yourself during online dating is to carry your cell phone on your person or other electronics like a smartwatch to the date just in case you need it for emergencies. In fact, have the speed dial ready for the authorities just in case you need to use it. That might seem far-fetched, but you just never know these days. in short, it is always good to have a Plan B just in case.

Online dating can be fun if you take certain precautions as to your welfare and safety. You must be aware at all times while trying to enjoy the company of your date. In fact, self-awareness is key to detecting if something just isn't right about the date you're experiencing. In short, listen to your intuition ladies. It is usually spot on. If something seems off during your date and you just don't feel comfortable, it is okay to walk away.

Another way to feel safer during an online date with somebody you just met off of Tinder is to have your friends nearby during your date. I don't mean to have them sitting so close to your date that they can listen in to the conversation, but perhaps have them in the immediate vicinity just in case. You will ultimately feel safer and assured this way. In other words, safety is the name if the game.

Chapter Summary

In this chapter, you have learned many ways to stay safe during online dating and just dating in general. You learned what to do and what not to do whilst finding the love of your life. And while you don't have to follow every single tip to staying safe during online dating, just putting into practice a few of these tips will ensure the safety and well-being of your person and your personal and private information. Just remember that online safety is synonymous with your personal safety. Some actions you can take to ensure your safety both online and offline during online dating are:

- Be aware.
- Don't give your private information away.
- Don't use sexually suggestive photos online.
- Don't give away your location.
- Reveal location to friends and family only.
- Drive yourself to and from the date to avoid your home address being known.
- Meet at a public place.
- Carry self-defense gadgets on your person.
- Don't leave your drink unattended.
- Don't get drunk.
- Research your online date.
- Don't use your full name in the dating app or social media.
- Ask your friends if they know the person.
- Use dating app's messaging feature.
- Go somewhere where security cameras are present.
- Have on speed dial the authorities.
- Listen to your intuition.

- Have personal friends nearby just in case.

There are also a few practical tasks that you can take action on to stay safe whilst online dating. These practical tasks will focus on what you can do right now to ensure your personal safety and security. For example, you can make a secure password to your personal Internet network by not using private information in your password like your birthdate or age. You can also ensure your safety online by using a nickname instead of your personal name in online dating profiles. In short, you can:

- Make a secure password to protect your Internet network.
- Use a nickname in your online dating profiles.
- Double check friend requests online to avoid somebody hacking into your account.

In the next chapter, you will learn if Mr. Right really exists out there. You will also learn that the stereotypical Mr. Right may not be everybody's cup of tea, but there may be a Mr. Right Now for you. This debate will be presented in a number of ways that are relevant to today's world.

Chapter Eleven: Does Mr. Right Really Exist?

It may be challenging to believe if there is a Mr. Right out there for you with all the risks associated with online dating and dating itself. The Internet itself can make it appear that Mr. Right may vaporize into thin air given the abstract nature of the online world and love. And since the nature of the Internet moves so fast, it can incline you to imagine that Mr. Right's existence is just as fleeting. In addition, given the stereotypical idealism and perfectionism associated with Mr. Right, a lot of women believe he does not exist. However, Mr. Right Now is very real.

Mr. Right Now may not be perfect, but he is perfect for you. In short, there is a piece for every puzzle waiting to be solved and sometimes if you are lucky, the pieces will fit together perfectly. However, sometimes Mr. Right just doesn't fit into your life for many reasons. Perhaps he or she is focused on being so perfect that a relationship in the real world beyond Ken and Barbie just doesn't work. In short, Mr. Right might be expending so much time and energy living up to that idealized image of perfection that he doesn't make the effort to reach for the perfect imperfections in another human being.

Be that as it may, many women often dream of Mr. Right. They dream he will magically sweep them off their feet with romance and excitement. Yet this is often unrealistic because as people become familiar with one another, reality sets in. And since this reality includes work, kids, and other responsibilities, who has the time or energy? Romance can sometimes be as elusive as Mr. Right himself it seems.

It would be more realistic to show small acts of favor and love rather than spend endless amounts of time and energy trying to engross somebody in a consuming romantic affair. Besides, what does it say when somebody tries to illicit your favor through repeated attempts at romance? It could mean he or she is only looking for one thing, sex. And that's not very romantic. In short, sometimes sex and love are two very different things.

On that note, it would seem the idea of Mr. Right is synonymous with romance. This may be because we watch all these romantic movies and comedies defining unrealistic expectations. Yet these unrealistic expectations of romance can pervade a woman's and a man's psyche to the point they try everything to live up to this notion of idealized romance. However, sometimes the person doing so ends up negating himself or herself in the process. This is not ideal for a real relationship.

However, what is real is Mr. Right Now's presence in your life. He may not be the most romantic guy, but he is present day after day. Beyond the initial romantic enticement, Mr. Right Now shows he cares for you by simply being present and available. Secondly, Mr. Right Now considers both you and himself in the relationship. In fact, it would seem Mr. Right Now is everything Mr. Right is not.

Actually, it seems that Mr. Right Now is the new Mr. Right. He is more grounded in reality and considers the relationship beyond a one-night stand. He realizes you both have needs and wants in real life that also requires attention and care. In short, Mr. Right Now realizes the big picture without negating the actors and directors in it.

On the other hand, Mr. Right is unrealistic because he tries to make love picture-perfect. This is not practical because the love shared between partners also has its ups and downs. And like any relationship, it can also have flaws and imperfections. This is because we are human, and thus fallible. In other words, love is perfectly imperfect.

I'm not saying Mr. Right does not exist, I'm simply saying to know what qualities you are looking for that would make a guy right for you. Don't succumb to some idealized, generic image of Mr. Right simply because you don't know what characteristics you want in a guy. Instead, note what essential qualities would make a guy a match for you, and go from there.

However, don't get so caught up looking for Mr. Right For You that you idealize him into something he is not. In fact, it would seem knowing what attracts you to another person can sometimes work against you because it sets you up into thinking there is nothing else out there that would be just as good for you regarding relationships. In short, women can sometimes think they are settling when they are not.

What women are reconciling is 'Mr. Right Now' for 'Mr. Right' because even Mr. Right may have trouble defining an idealized love. He may define it through actions like buying flowers and words like 'I love you.' However, love can be defined as it is what you make it day after day. It is this reality that entails many actions and words beyond romance.

Perhaps Mr. Right would be a more concrete reality if love were a more tangible thing than a box of chocolates on Valentine's day. The reason Mr. Right has such a hard time defining love is that emotions and feelings cannot be bottled up like some fragrance he or she might give you as a gift. Instead, they have a reality of their own that defies definition, as it is more than just one thing, word, or action. In short, love is the entire realm of the emotional, mental, and physical realities shared between partners.

I had my experience with Mr. Right years ago, and the result was I got hurt and disappointed because all the relationship seemed to be about was gratifying each other's immediate physical needs. In short, each other's needs and emotions were not considered in the long run along with the fact that we were both stationed outside of the U.S. at the time and were only looking for comfort pillows in response to being halfway around the world outside of the home. When the time came to get stationed elsewhere and separate from each other, my heart broke in not having that immediate comfort available to me. Lesson learned, albeit the hard way.

It would seem that in order for Mr. Right to exist, there needs to be a Ms. Right. One cannot exist without the other, and everything I said about Mr. Right also applies to Ms. Right as well. The door swings both ways as both must learn the difference between personifying love and loving a person day-in and day-out. However, romance and love can co-exist if both partners consider more than the present moment.

Likewise, Mr. Right Now may not be everybody's cup of tea, and that's okay. Some people may want immediate romance as compared to getting to know somebody first. It just depends on what you are looking for in a mate. Once again, it comes down to which characteristics and attributes that make Mr. Right Now realistically feasible.

In fact, it would seem that Mr. Right and Mr. Right Now could learn a thing or two from each other. Perhaps the romantic Mr. Right could become more grounded in reality while the realistic Mr. Right Now remembers to surprise his lady every once in a while with tulips. It is this sought-after combination that ladies dream of. Maybe they can have it all.

Be that as it may, the perfect guy for you is alive out there somewhere. You just have to step up and be what you want to attract, whether that is Mr. Right or Mr. Right Now. In short, embody and exude the characteristics, qualities, and attributes you want in another, and you might just find your mate after all. Like attracts like.

Another reason Mr. Right may not as prevalent in today's society is that women generally don't want to take the time to train him to be Mr. Right. In other words, a potential love interest doesn't want to expend energy teaching Mr. Right to love himself, herself, and potentially other women in the future. Women these days are very busy with their own lives. Be that as it may, perhaps Mr. Right Now can be taught how to love you through your kindness and patience with him.

On that note, perhaps Mr. Right Now is elusive because he is busy with his own life, instead of trying to live up to the double-standards and expectations heaped onto him. Yes, even men have double-standards heaped onto them. It is almost like the penis-penalty, as some ladies expect the guy to pay simply because he is the guy. How unrealistic is that? This surely doesn't help Mr. Right's case either.

However, if Mr. Right had more confidence in himself as compared to succumbing to a romantic stereotype, perhaps he might be more readily available to the ladies. This is because of Mr. Right taking the time to work on himself inwardly, as compared to an external reason like his physique for self-improvement. After all, real confidence comes from within, and not from without. The same goes for the ladies.

On the other hand, Mr. Right Now's confidence in himself and his abilities is why he is so sexy and attractive to you. He may not know everything yet that there is to know about loving you, but his intrinsic confidence will carry him through, as compared to Mr. Right's brief flash of confidence in moves that have been around for years. In short, Mr. Right's time has come and gone, so why not give Mr. Right Now a chance?

Chapter Summary

In this chapter, you have learned why Mr. Right is so elusive. In addition, you have learned some main differences between Mr. Right and Mr. Right Now. This information will help you decide what it is you want in a partner as you traverse the sea of dating, romance, and love. Lastly, you have learned that although Mr. Right is a thing of the past, you have also learned that there may be a Mr. Right Now for you.

In short, Mr. Right Now for you:

- May not be perfect compared to Mr. Right.
- Understands the differences between sex and love.
- Is mindfully present and available.
- Is more grounded to reality.
- Understands love is perfectly imperfect.
- Understands love is the entire realm of emotional, mental, and physical reality.
- Considers more than immediate needs in the present moment.
- Understands the difference between personifying love and loving you.
- Will eventually understand how to love you.
- Has real confidence in himself and you.

There are also a few practical tasks that you can take action to finding Mr. Right Now. These practical tasks will focus on what you can do in this moment to find Mr. Right Now. For example, you can sign up for typically male-oriented classes where he might be already. You could also go where guys will generally be hanging out, like gyms or some other place. In short, you can:

- Sign up for typically male-oriented classes.
- Go where guys will generally be hanging out.
- Hook up through a friend of a friend.

Conclusion

It would seem that dating, romance, and love are part nature and nurture because one's internal climate can influence and affect his or her external environment through variables such as emotion and an existing status-quo like the Information Age. In short, the times and how it influences us matters because it affects both our internal state and our outward actions. However, we can take action to minimize this susceptibility in the quest for love. In short, love seems to always land on its feet through the perpetual action and reaction involved in balancing our physical, emotional, and mental equilibrium with one another. It is this ultimate human connection that empowers us beyond the electronics we contend with daily.

This human connection empowers us to make choices that can improve our lives with romance and love as we intermingle an old-fashioned romance with the new reality of the here and now of dating apps and matchmaking websites. Be that as it may, it would seem there are still precautions to take whilst online dating and even organic dating these days. Since both your personal and private information is on the Internet for all to see, personal safety and well-being are utmost in importance because what you do online can affect what you do offline and vice versa. It would seem acting in the best interest of yourself and of those you love takes on a whole new meaning as the human connection almost becomes a thing of the past given the pervasiveness of electronics.

On the other hand, electronics likes tablets and cell phones can also aid the human connection in pushing us towards dating, romance, and love. For example, we can decide who we like and don't like by showcasing our best self on online dating profiles in the hopes a potential love interest will swipe right on a dating app like Tinder. In short, online dating apps and websites make it too easy to find the love of your life. Is this is the case, then why do we struggle so much with dating, romance, and love itself? Perhaps we have forgotten the essential ingredients of relationships themselves by the means of the Internet making everything so readily available and obvious.

However, not obvious nor written in stone anymore are things like how to find the perfect partner, the art of attraction, and ways to maintain and improve your relationship. This is less obvious because relationships and love itself are always evolving from one moment to the next. In short, every relationship is uniquely different given the unique people in it, and their way of interacting with one another. It is this evolving interaction that could benefit from a few general tips and advice. Tips and advice like be your best self apply to all stages of a relationship as it is never static.

A relationship incorporates the emotional, physical, and mental reality that defines the shared experience for both partners. This human connection perpetuates the relationship while keeping it balanced and stable. However, sometimes things get off track. This is when you return to the basics in remembering what attracted you love birds in the first place. Advice like working together as a team is invaluable because it is the glue that holds the relationship together through the thick and thin. It is this shared experience that allows for everything in the relationship to flourish and thrive into something bigger than either person.

Yet it is the individuals' actions in the relationship that determines the direction and future of it. Actions, like being authentic and pacing yourself during a date, can initiate the flow of the relationship itself as you show and demonstrate what you want and consequently don't want from it. Secondly, taking action like communicating with your potential love interest shows you are not some passive wallflower just letting things happen to you during a date and in the possible future relationship. It shows you are indeed mindfully present and actively engaging with the whole process of dating and relationships.

However even the most stable of relationships could use a little help sometimes. Often times, we get so busy with responsibilities that we forget to invest in each other. Advice like simply talking and making time for one another can improve your relationship tenfold. Even working on chores together can increase not only the time you spend together but also the likelihood you talk to each other about what's on your minds. Whether it's through words or body language, communication is key to improving and maintaining your relationship.

However, communication begins with you. From communicating online through texting in the dating app's messaging feature to communicating organically on your first date, your words and actions are like a feedback loop of sorts informing your potential love interest of your thoughts, feelings, and intentions. It is this transfer of information that is vital to not only the date but also to the possible future relationship between you two. And while you want to be self-aware and mindfully present, you also want to let it happen naturally. After all, human nature is what brought you two together in the first place.

However, the nature of dating, romance, and relationships is somewhat altered by the presence of the Internet. It seems we no longer go out on regular dates anymore given the plethora of personally identifying information available online. Instead of organically asking our date what he or she likes, all we have to do is look on his or her online dating profile to determine such things. This can be a setup, however, because we go into the date with certain preconceived notions and expectations, in effect profiling the date before it even happens. This is why it is important to get back to organic dating.

Organic dating means you put away your electronics and fully engage your date in the here and now. It means you make eye contact and actually have a meaningful conversation with each other as compared to texting each other on your cellphones during the date. In short, you take the time to get to know your date the old-fashioned way through an interactive expression of body language and words. It is this way of organic dating that is more intuitive that speed dating through your laptop. In short, the other party has to be present as well.

It would seem being present on a date and in a relationship can take on a whole new meaning as we might exaggerate the communicative interactions to compensate for the presence of electronics in our lives. In short, we are all living our best lives as a result. It is this pattern of living that suggests balance is needed now more than ever with moderation in all aspects of our lives, even our love lives. Yet the presence of Mr. Right might infer otherwise as he showers us with gifts and adoration. In fact, it would seem the common infatuation with Mr. Right in comparison to Mr. Right Now suggests how unbalanced things can be in a relationship and in life if we overdo it in any one aspect.

We have to be more adaptable to varying environments, realities, and milieus if we want a relationship to work. Realities like dating, romance, and love, for example, should supersede all others because, without the human connection, all other environments become meaningless. In other words, the Internet and your electronics can't love you back like the love of your life can. This human interaction is life itself, hence the need for this book.

In this book, you have learned the importance of being an active participant in dating, romance, and relationships. You have learned advice and tips to incline this romantic interaction to come to fruition in your own life. By applying the knowledge within, your love life will improve greatly and become a sustaining presence that carries you and your love through anything. Just remember to invest in this book and each other from time to time to keep that spark alive.

In order to keep that spark alive, just remember to apply the tips and advice in each chapter. In short, just don't read the material, but do something about it to change the situation for the better. For example, chapter one on "Why Modern Dating Is Challenging And How To Fix It," implies that even with all the available technology at our fingertips, you should:

- Take care of yourself.
- Stay true to yourself.
- Keep it real.
- Don't sweat the small stuff.
- Relax and have fun!

More practical actions you can take to navigating modern dating are also:

- Check out dating apps and websites..
- Research which dating app or website is best suited for you personally.
- Talk to others about their online dating stories and experiences.

Yet even with all the challenges of modern dating like the Internet detracting from some of our individual volition and agency, chapter two on "Are You Dating Confident?," gives very actionable steps to take the power back to become a dating superstar. In order to date confidently and assuredly, you should:

- Being confident starts with you.
- Be your own first date!
- Trust yourself.
- Self-love and self-respect are vital.
- Be realistic.
- Be open to new experiences.
- Take care of yourself.
- Don't reveal too much, leave a little to the imagination.
- Let it happen naturally.
- Don't compare yourself to others.
- Give your date your full attention.
- Communicate!

More practical actions you can take to dating confident are also:

- Work on body image and confidence by joining a gym or team sport..
- Work on social skills by getting out and socializing more.
- Read up on current dating trends.

Even if you are dating confident, finding your ideally perfect partner presents a whole new set of challenges like how to take dating to the next level in a possible relationship. In short, dating becomes a way of life if you are serious about finding the love of your life. Chapter three on "How To Find The Perfect Partner," gives many steps you can undertake to achieve this. For example, you can remember:

- Offline dating and courting are more authentic and genuine.
- Leave your preconceived notions and dating conventions at the door.
- Go socialize and hang out someplace less expected to meet Mr. Right.
- Give Mr. Right your time and energy.
- Stay true to yourself but work on your flaws and interests.
- Be happy and satisfied with what you already have.
- Just let it be; if it's meant to be, it's meant to be.
- Be honest, upfront, and straightforward.
- Avoid playing games.
- Apply your intelligence and wit and think for yourself.
- Be willing to learn from your mistakes.
- And just try your best!

More practical actions you can take to finding the perfect partner are also:

- Ask friends and family to help you in your mission of finding the perfect partner.
- Invite people over for informal get-togethers like a bonfire with friends of friends.
- Join a bigger community to meet new people like the Red Cross.

Clearly, finding your perfect partner would be much more challenging without knowledge about the art of attraction. Chapter four on "The Art Of Attraction," gives much advice on how to woo and attract your ideal mate. From everything to looking your best to using your body language to indicate mutual interest, you will know what the art of attraction is and is not. In short, the art of attraction is:

- A mutual desire to be closer to your love interest.
- Liking the entire package of emotional, physical, and intellectual attributes.
- Both dynamic and interactive.
- The confidence to be your best self and to always improve.
- A reciprocal give-and-take of mutual interest in each other.
- Not controlling the outcome and letting it happen naturally.
- Doing favors for each other.
- Feeling both needed and wanted.
- Taking the time to earn one's trust and confidence with careful attention to detail.
- The human connection that results from your attempt to woo and attract.

More practical actions you can take as to the art of attraction are also:

- Make personal hygiene a must.
- Practice flirting with a friend.
- Give compliments often.

The art of attraction also becomes apparent when you are trying to date online via a dating app like Tinder. Since dating online is relatively new and therefore not set in stone, chapter five on "Online Dating & Tinder: The Masterplan," give you very actionable tips you can assimilate yourself. These actionable tips will help you master the online dating world if you remember to:

- To be yourself when it comes to online dating.
- Don't wait too long to take the relationship offline.
- Don't reveal too much in your online dating profile.
- Write about what you want in a potential love interest.
- Upload a nice photo of yourself.
- Make your online conversation interesting and not dull.

- Don't take the online dating experience too seriously.
- Don't become disheartened.
- Initiate the conversation.
- Have other methods of meeting people besides online.
- Step out of your comfort zone via online dating.
- Realize your worth.
- Don't give out too much personal information online.
- Watch out for scam artists.
- Don't rush into it.
- Don't critique or judge your online love interest.
- Find a potential love interest with similar goals.
- Take the time to get to know your potential love interest.
- Be timely in your online dating responses.
- Stand out amongst the herd with your online profile.
- Use dating apps and matchmaking websites like Tinder to your advantage.

More practical actions you can take as to online dating are also:

- Fill out online profile at more than one dating app or matchmaking website.
- Like as many love interests as you can to drive results you get for similar online interests.
- Ask a friend for an objective opinion on your online dating profile.

Since online dating apps like Tinder and matchmaking websites like eHarmony are still in the works, it is advisable to return to organic dating to get to know that somebody special. Yet in order to do so, one must learn very valuable dating tips. Chapter six on "Dating Tips You Need To Know," implies dating can be fun if you:

- Are authentic and genuine.
- Take the lead and initiate conversation.

- Use your body language to infer interest.
- Know your limits on alcoholic drinks.
- Don't expect to be wined and dined.
- Wear classic clothing pieces.
- Don't mention your ex.
- Put away your electronics.
- Show you are playful and fun.
- Don't turn your date into a research project before you meet him.
- Leave your preconceived notions at the door.
- Let him pay the bill if he chooses.
- Are honest.
- Keep it short and sweet.
- Put yourself in the right frame of mind ahead of time.
- Burn off some of that nervous energy beforehand.
- Are Mindful.
- Give plenty of eye contact.
- Discuss what you're passionate about with your date.
- Have fun and pace yourself.

More practical actions you can take to dating itself are also:

- Practice talking to your date in front of a mirror before the date itself.
- Go on a group date first.
- Sign up for a speed-dating outing to get more experience with dating itself.

Many people think dating grinds to a halt when you get in a serious relationship. However, you still need to connect as a couple to make the relationship work. And date nights are a very good idea for any couple. Chapter seven on, "Eight Easy Ways To Maintain & Improve Your Relationship," gives suggestions on how to sustain and enhance an already viable relationship. Some of these suggestions are to:

- Love yourself.
- Be supportive.
- Be accepting of his friends.
- Be spontaneous.
- Make time for hot sex.
- Connect physically, emotionally, and mentally.
- Communicate.
- Work together as a team.

More practical actions to take in maintaining and improving your relationship are also:

- Plan a mini vacation weekend for the two of you.
- Surprise your love with a meaningful gift.
- Make yourself available to offer your help or services if needed.

Yet even if your relationship is thriving and flourishing, there are still some common relationship challenges every couple faces at one time or another. Chapter eight on, "Seven Common Relationship Challenges (And How To Fix Them)," not only discusses the challenges themselves but also presents workable solutions to those relationship challenges. Just remember to:

- Talk.
- Take Action.
- Make time for each other.
- Have lots of good sex!
- Be honest about money.
- Do chores together.

- Work on conflict resolution.

More practical actions to take in navigating relationship challenges are also:

- Actively listen.
- Ask for clarification.
- Repeat back to your partner what he or she has expressed to you..

Another challenge to any relationship is to learn how to date whether you're just beginning the relationship or currently in one. Dating can be fun if we learn not to take it so seriously and just relax. In fact, chapter nine on, "How To Date And Actually Enjoy It," suggests dating is a fun process and experience regardless of your position in the relationship. Dating can be fun if you;

- Mindfully be at the moment.
- Pace yourself.
- Pay attention.
- Expect the unexpected.
- Use your five senses.
- Don't take it so seriously.
- Learn and experience a new skill or hobby together.
- Go out on more date.
- Go out on dates with other couples.
- Be less judgemental.
- Have manners.
- Be yourself.
- Don't have an unrealistic expectation.
- Let your hair down and have fun.
- Be receptive to new ideas and suggestions.
- Be imaginative and original.

More practical actions to take as to how to date and actually enjoy it are also:

- Say or do something to break the ice.
- Enact small gestures of kindness like opening the door for your date..
- Genuinely smile and laugh on a date.

Organic dating is clearly fun and an engaging process and experience for everyone involved. However, online dating can also be precarious in that your safety, security, and well-being could be at risk with the abundance of personal and private information online. In Chapter ten, "How To Stay Safe Whilst Online Dating," gives very actionable steps to protect yourself amidst a sea of questionable sharks. For example, you can:

- Be aware.
- Don't give your private information away.
- Don't use sexually suggestive photos online.
- Don't give away your location.
- Reveal location to friends and family only.
- Drive yourself to and from the date to avoid your home address being known.
- Meet at a public place.
- Carry self-defense gadgets on your person.
- Don't leave your drink unattended.
- Don't get drunk.
- Research your online date.
- Don't use your full name in the dating app or social media.
- Ask your friends if they know the person.
- Use dating app's messaging feature.
- Go somewhere where security cameras are present.
- Have on speed dial the authorities.

- Listen to your intuition.
- Have personal friends nearby just in case.

More practical actions you can take to stay safe whilst online dating are also:

- Make a secure password to protect your Internet network.
- Use a nickname in your online dating profiles.
- Double check friend requests online to avoid somebody hacking into your account.

With all the risks associated with online dating and dating itself, it seems Mr. Right is just as momentary and fleeting as the nature of the Internet and love itself. In fact, Mr. Right is a very outdated analogy of an idealized perfect romance that is fading from society because the reality is very few have time for a consuming romantic affair given work, kids, and other responsibilities. Be that as it may, chapter eleven on, "Does Mr. Right Really Exist?," suggests that Mr. Right Now is more feasible given he is more adaptable to many realities and environments whereas Mr. Right just focuses on one. In short Mr. Right Now:

- May not be perfect compared to Mr. Right.
- Understands the differences between sex and love.
- Is mindfully present and available.
- Is grounded in reality.
- Understands love is perfectly imperfect.
- Understands love is the entire realm of emotional, mental, and physical reality.
- Considers more than immediate needs in the present moment.
- Understands the difference between personifying love and loving you.
- Will eventually understand how to love you.

- Has real confidence in himself and you.

More practical actions you can take to finding Mr. Right Now are to also:

- Sign up for typically male-oriented classes.
- Go where guys will generally be hangout out.
- Hook up through a friend of a friend.

Just remember to have fun and to be yourself with dating, romance and love, and the men will be at your doorstep practically breaking the door down to get to know the beautiful person that is you. You are unique, special, and one-of-a-kind, so treat yourself like you are your own first date. Continually invest and love yourself, and people will love you for you.

www.ingramcontent.com/pod-product-compliance
Lightning Source LLC
Chambersburg PA
CBHW071003080526
44587CB00015B/2330